AUGUSTE RODIN

Lay-out by Lionel Scanteye

Translated by
Kathleen Muston and Geoffrey Skelding

© Editions du Musée Rodin, Paris, 1990

I.S.B.N. 2-901428-28-2

IONEL JIANOU

RODIN

Forword by
C. GOLDSCHEIDER

forword

With more and more young people finding pleasure in visits to Galleries and Museums, the need has been felt for a wider distribution of books about art. This new public demands high standards both of text and illustration, but cannot afford anything too expensive. Arted, true to its twin cultural aims of making art available to all and opening up more paths to knowledge, is reissuing in a new format its famous series on the great sculptors of our time.

The history of modern sculpture begins with Auguste Rodin (1840-1917). The approach devised by Professor Ionel Jianou in this book explains the artist's achievements, his influence on others, and the character of an art that attained universality by remaining human.

The section on his work as a sculptor shows how it was that Rodin was able to win a series of victories over the spirit of his time — an age in which art had to conform to outmoded routines and conventions in order to get official recognition. It reveals how exacting Rodin was as he wrestled with the difficulties of his craft : the quantity of sketches and models accumulated in his studios is truly amazing, both for portraits and for what were to become famous monuments like The Burghers of Calais, Victor Hugo, and Balzac.

From the moment he asserted a character opposed to academic tradition, Rodin enjoyed the support and confidence of a small group of friends capable of appreciating original talent. Shy and sensitive to hostile criticism, he left others to defend him, while each new creation from The Age of Bronze in 1877 to Balzac in 1898 brought a fresh wave of attacks. At the same time he was beginning to attract the attention of recognized connoisseurs and collectors such as Karl Jacobsen in Denmark, Max Linde and August Thyssen in Germany, Mrs Simpson and Thomas Ryan in the United States. They spread Rodin's fame far from his own country and enriched Galleries and Museums with their collections. Rodin's death did not arrest the impetus thus given. Two great collections were made of sculptures, drawings, and water-colours : one, Jules Mastbaum's, founded the Rodin Museum of Philadelphia ; the other, Matsukata Kojiro's, was presented to the Tokyo Museum of Western Art, designed by Le Corbusier, the showplace of French art in the Far East.

More recent collections and numerous exhibitions in France and elsewhere demonstrate that Rodin's work has assumed ever growing significance with the passage of time, has become increasingly an integral part of contemporary life. Rodin's name has become a household word, as famous as that of Michelangelo.

C. GOLDSCHEIDER

Rodin's struggle

*Intelligence designs
but the heart does the modelling.*

Rodin

No artist was more contested or more insulted than Rodin. No artist had more ardent and faithful admirers. The fierce battle that raged around his work lasted forty years, from the campaign against his statue *The Age of Bronze* in 1877 to the efforts in 1916 to prevent the creation of the Musée Rodin.

Anatole France wrote in 1900 : 'Insult and outrage are the wages of genius and Rodin after all only got his fair share.' [1]

None of this 'fair share' was spared him. His most famous monuments — *The Burghers of Calais, Victor Hugo, Claude Lorrain* and *Sarmiento* — encountered severe opposition. His statue of *Balzac* — rejected in 1898 by the *Société des Gens de Lettres* — unleashed attacks of the utmost violence. Rodin was derisively nicknamed 'the Michelangelo of the goitre'. The statue was described as 'a magnificent monster, a scarecrow, the mask of a rabid cat', 'a mental aberration', 'a block that disgraces its author and French art.' [2]

1. Anatole France : La Porte de l'Enfer, Le Figaro, 7-6-1900.

2. J.-E. Blanche : La Vie Artistique sous la IIIᵉ République, 1931; Jean Rameau : La victoire de M. Rodin, Le Gaulois, May 1898; A. Flament : Les Riches amateurs, La Presse, 19-5-1898.

In November 1916, when the artist, aged 76, was at the height of his fame, a speaker still ventured to declare in the Senate : 'What really is this Mr. Rodin and what is his art ? Demented, hallucinated, possessed, convulsive or a humbug, Mr. Rodin claims to have enriched and even renewed art. It is a rebellion against form, order and balance, against sanity, reason and tradition, against good taste and common sense !' [3]

These violent insults reveal what was at stake : the renewal of art to give back to sculpture the integrity of form and to the artist the freedom to create.

The order that Rodin rebelled against was the academic order, whose dogmas, conventions, pomposity and mawkishness has perverted the great traditions of French sculpture.

In his *Homage to Rodin,* Brancusi said : 'Ever since Michelangelo sculptors had been striving to be grandiose but succeeded only to be grandiloquent. In the nineteenth century, sculpture was in a desperate state. Rodin came along and changed everything. Thanks to him, Man became the unit of measurement of sculptural conception. Thanks to him, sculpture became human again, both in scale and content. Rodin's influence was and still is tremendous. [4]

Rodin's rebellion corresponds to that of his friends and contemporaries, the impressionist painters : it has the same causes and, with a few differences, the same character. But whereas the impressionists formed a group to champion their ideas, Rodin was alone in his fight to renew sculpture.

In a report on the occasion of the 1900 World Exhibition, Leonce Benedite wrongly proclaimed that

3. G. Coquiot : Rodin à l'Hôtel Biron, Ed. Ollendorf, 1917, p. 186.

4. C. Brancusi : Hommage à Rodin, Catalogue du 4e Salon de la Jeune Sculpture, Paris, 1954.

'statuary art escaped the vicissitudes that marked the development of 19th century painting'. But he was right in adding that 'one does not properly speaking find rival schools, and efforts to break the grip of despotic and obsolete dogmas were made by isolated individuals.' [5]

The 'isolated individuals' were Rude, Barye, Carpeaux and Rodin. The first three were crushed by the numbers and power of their adversaries, but Rodin finally emerged triumphant and so paved the way for modern sculpture in the 20th century.

To understand just how great a victory it was, we need to go back a hundred years and consider the situation of French sculpture under Napoleon III.

Sculptors, at that time, had only three ways by which to assert themselves : exhibiting at the *Salon des Artistes Français,* winning great competitions and securing contracts for public monuments or the decoration of public buildings.

The *Salon des Artistes Français,* founded in 1673, was the only official exhibition existing at the time of Napoleon III. The unofficial 'Salons' began only later, first the *Salon des Artistes Indépendants* in 1884, followed in 1890 by the *Salon de la Société Nationale des Beaux-Arts,* of which Rodin was a founder. It was after 1880 that art galleries began to exhibit sculpture and Rodin was one of the first to have a special exhibition of his works in one, in 1889.

If a sculptor was refused access to the *Salon des Artistes Français,* he had practically no other means of making his works known, except by exhibiting them at his own cost.

The selection board of the *Salon des Artistes Français* was composed of members of the French

5. L. Bénédite : La Sculpture in Rapports du Jury International à l'Exposition Universelle de 1900, p. 533.

Institute, determined to keep out all artistic innovation.

The Salon of 1863 rejected over four thousand works. To placate the indignant artists, who included Manet, Whistler, Jongkind, Pissarro, Guillaumin and Cezanne, Napoleon III decided to hold a separate exhibition for them. This — the *Salon des Refusés* — had a considerable impact despite an unfriendly press and public derision. It started the decline of the academic school, whose hold on artistic life was challenged for the first time.

It was the same for Government competitions and orders. The champions of academic art held the key-positions and awarded the prizes and contracts to their favourites.

When Rude had finished his high-relief the *Marseillaise* for the Arc de Triomphe in Paris, his enemies denigrated the masterpiece saying 'the face of Liberty as shown by Rude is hideous'. They succeeded by their intrigues in securing for Etex the order for the other groups of the Arc de Triomphe. In the same way, they prevented Barye's *Lion* being bought for the Tuileries Garden. One of his colleagues exclaimed : 'Are we to turn the Tuileries into a zoo ? The day this horror is put in a public place, it is to be hoped the crowd will not leave a crumb of it !' [6]

In 1878, it was not Rodin but Barrias who won the competition for the *Defence of Paris Monument* at Courbevoie. Rodin failed in four other competitions between 1879 and 1881.

When he showed *The Age of Bronze* and the plaster cast of *St. John the Baptist preaching* at the *Salon des Artistes Français,* the first prize went to Jean-Antoine Idrac and to René de Saint-

6. Arsène Alexandre : Le Balzac de Rodin, Ed. Floury, 1898.

Marceaux. Five second-prizes were awarded, thirteen third-prizes and fifteen honourable mentions. On page XVI of the Catalogue of the *Salon des Artistes Français* for 1880, Rodin is among those who received honourable mention. This was the only reward he received up to 1889 when he stopped entering for the *Salon des Artistes Français*. But people like Jean Turcan, Emile-Joseph Carlier, A. Cordonnier, Jules-Félix Coutan, Laurent-Honoré Marquest, Paul-Armand de la Vingtrie, Hector Lemaire, Léon Longepied, J.B. Hugues, Anatole Marquet de Vasselot and many other sculptors now completely forgotten won the prizes that Rodin was refused.

These rewards were intended to establish a hierarchy in the world of art. At the apex were the *Great Masters,* members of the Institut, professors at the *Ecole Supérieure des Beaux-Arts,* holders of all distinctions and honours, beneficiaries of all official stipends. Then came their disciples, waiting to replace them and in the meantime enjoying their protection. In the third rank were the other artists, self-taught or self-willed, who refused to follow the beaten tracks and 'the despotic and obsolete dogmas' of the Academy.

The first aim of Rodin and the impressionist painters was to get the privileges of the hierarchy abolished and restore the independence of artists. Their rebellion was thus professional, social and moral in character. They claimed that they were continuing the great traditions of French art and in no way saw themselves as revolutionaries.

In his *History of Impressionism,* John Rewald states : 'these painters in reality genuinely continued the works and theories of their predecessors. So that this new phase in the history of art was

7. John Rewald : Histoire de l'Impressionnisme, Albin Michel, 1955, p. 8.

8. Conversations with Rodin, Le Matin, 13-7-1908.

not truly a sudden outburst of revolutionary tendencies, but rather the culmination of a slow and perfectly logical development.' [7]

Rodin himself said : 'I have forged a link between my own times and the great traditions of the past. I strenghten that link every day.' [8]

To show their ties with their forerunners, they did not hesitate to enter their names in the Catalogues of the Salon as disciples of the *Great Masters* Thus, Pissarro is entered as 'student of Mr. A.L. Melbye'; Renoir, Bazille and Sisley as 'student of Mr. Gleyre', and Rodin as 'student of Mr. Carrier-Belleuse'.

However, they reinterpreted the old traditions, striving to revitalize them and to relate them to the spirit of the times.

That was the main thing that separated them from the academics, cramped in a fixed interpretation of traditions, regardless of the changes in French society and the new ideas about art that necessarily flowed from those changes.

Rodin and the impressionists were the first generation of artists to assert themselves under the Third Republic.

The liberal middle classes, who had opposed the despotism of Napoleon III, came to power after the disastrous war of 1870 and the tragedy of the *Commune.* Enriched by the industrial revolution, economic expansion and financial speculation, these middle-class liberals were not bound by tradition. Positivists, determined to enjoy the present to the full, with an unshakable faith in evolution and progress, they were more interested in the future's promise than in relics of the past. Like the burghers of the Golden Age of Holland, they wanted a realistic art in which they could see the reflection of their own success.

The mythological and historical subjects of the academics were ill attuned to the tastes and aspirations of this rapidly rising new class. Realists in their enterprises and speculations, they expected art to be true and draw its inspiration from contemporary life.

Courbet announced his programme as early as 1855 : 'To translate the manners, ideas and aspects of my time as I see them, in short to produce living art.' [9]

About the same time, Fernand Desnoyers proclaimed : 'Let us write or paint only what is or at least what we see, what we know, what we live... A strange school, no doubt, which has neither master nor disciples and whose only rules are *independence, sincerity* and *individualism.*' [10]

Rodin and the impressionists nourished these ideas. To apply them, they sought the most appropriate means and thus came to invent a new language of art completely opposed to that of the academic school.

Rodin said : 'The artist is the seer. He is the man whose eyes are open and to whose spirit the inner essence of things is made known, at any rate, as a fact of existence... I reproduce only what I have seen and what anyone else could see if they would take the trouble; but then I am always looking and I know there remains to be found out infinitely more than I shall ever have time to discover.' [11]

In his work, feeling comes before theory, sensation and emotion before established rules. Rodin is an artist who can see and dares to

9. G. Courbet : Le Réalisme, see J. Rewald, p. 22.

10 F Desnoyers : Du Réalisme, see J. Rewald, p. 42.

11. Conversations with Rodin, in F. Lawton : A. Rodin, F. Fischer Unwin, 1906, p. 158.

12. A. Rodin - Paul Gsell. L'Art, Entretiens réunis par Paul Gsell, Grasset, 1951, p. 47.

13. A. Rodin : Pensées, L'Art et les Artistes, nr. 109, 1914, p. 37-40.

14. Conversations with Rodin, in F. Lawton, p. 160.

express in all sincerity what he has seen. He discovers the enchantment of light and its resources, the vibration and intimate movement of surfaces and planes, the throb of passion that animates form. He uses 'high lights, heavy shadows, paleness, quivering, vaporous half-tones, and transitions so finely shaded that they seem to dissolve into air', giving his sculpture 'the radiance of living flesh.' [12]

He loves life : 'Sculpture does not need to be original, what it needs is life', he says. [13] And to him life means movement, action.

'I used to think that movement was the chief thing in sculpture and in all I did it was what I tried to attain. My *Gates of Hell* is the record of these strivings... There I have made movement yield all it can.' [14]

But he does not think of movement simply as the transition from one attitude to another, a gesture or the shifting of an object in space. Movement is a way of expressing inner life, it is the emotional impulse that causes his sculptures to thrill and surge from within.

15. A. Rodin - Paul Gsell, p. 64.

'Grief, joy, thoughts — in our art all becomes action', he said. [15]

Movement foments and exalts matter : it is the subjective drive that animates objective form. All feeling is expressed by an inner movement.

Movement also signifies becoming. The concept of time joins that of space, giving a new dimension to the work of art.

16. G. Simmel : l'Œuvre de Rodin comme expression de l'esprit moderne, Mélanges de philosophie relativiste, F. Alcan, 1912, p. 132-133.

The fleeting impression of an ephemeral aspect, captured in all its freshness, is made permanent by the artist. The active character of artistic creation is the result of this conflict between opposites : duration and becoming.

The conflict between permanence and becoming is matched by the conflict between substance and mobility. Rodin's contribution was to find a new balance between these opposites.

In 1900, the German philosopher Georg Simmel noted : By inventing a new flexibility of joints, giving surfaces a new tone and vibration, suggesting in a new way the contact of two bodies or parts of the same body, using a new distribution of light by means of clashing, conflicting or corresponding planes Rodin has given to the human figure a new mobility which reveals the inner life of man, his feelings, thoughts and personal vicissitudes more completely than was ever possible before... What characterizes this modern age is the tendency to live and interpret the world according to the reactions of our inner life, the dissolution of solid content in the fluid of the perfectly insubstantial soul, whose forms 'can only be forms of movement.'[16]

To express in sculpture the new balance between duration and becoming, substance and mobility, Rodin used three processes which shocked his contemporaries : composition, *unfinished form* and modelling from within.

'Great artists (he said) proceed as Nature *composes,* not as anatomy describes. They do not carve a particular muscle or nerve or bone for its own sake. They see and express the whole and by broad planes their work throbs with light or sinks into shade... The expression of life, to preserve the infinite suppleness of reality, must never be frozen and fixed.' [17]

This concept of composition is best explained by contrast with construction. Composition leads

to a balance of forces, construction to a balance of masses. One is like music in orchestration of harmonies and concordances, the other like architecture in disposition of volumes. In composition a plane is seen in relation to the whole, in construction in relation to other planes. Composition suggests motion and 'the infinite suppleness of reality', while construction achieves the solid structure of finite static forms.

THE THREE SHADES.
*Group intended to overhang
the Gates of Hell.*

The only admirable forms are the appropriate forms, those that call for and imply one another, with the irrefutable logic of harmonious necessity, those that draw life one from the other. One detail not in harmony with all the rest, the slightest discord among profiles, and the masterpiece will be destroyed, a useless object, a structure that light denies, doomed to be everything barren and harsh.' [18]

17-18. A. Rodin : A la Venus de Milo, l'Art et les Artistes, nr. 109, 1914, p. 91-104.

Composition assembles the diverse aspects of life according to the demands of an inner harmonious necessity. Diversity represents the ephemeral aspects of becoming. Only the Wole aspires to permanence, because it is fulfillment.

By this union of becoming and duration, art 'advances to the preserve of the Unknowable.' [19]

19-20. A. Rodin - Paul Gsell, p. 145-146.

'Great works of art say all that can be said about man and the world, and then convey that there is something more that cannot be known. Every masterpiece has this quality of mystery.' [20]

Rodin's sculpture approaches the Unknowable and make us realise its existence. There is no art without mystery or without poetry.

The 'leaving unfinished' technique helps to express better the mystery of form awakening in the stone. Every artist reaches the point where he feels he must go no further; to give his work more finishing touches would only deprive it of life. Rodin dared to stop at that point and often left uncut stone around a form. In this way he allows us to assist at the birth of form as it comes into being and awakens to life. A movement is caught in its intimate process and we feel it will progressively unfold according to an ineluctable necessity.

For this bold technique, Rodin was accused of being unable to finish his works. He upset the teaching of the Academy, but he endowed sculpture with a new poetic function by 'discerning between what was and was is to be.' [21]

21. A. Rodin - Paul Gsell, p. 54.

The third process used by Rodin in order to give more life to his sculptures was modelling 'in depth' or from within.

In his conversations with Paul Gsell, he tells how an old stone-carver taught him the art of modelling : 'Always remember what I am going to say. Henceforth when you carve, never see forms in breadth, but always in depths... Never consider a surface as anything but the extremity of a volume, the point more or less large it directs towards you. That way you will learn the art of modelling. 'And Rodin adds : 'This principle was astonishingly fruitful to me. I applied it to the execution of figures. Instead of imagining the parts of a body as more or less flat surfaces, I represented them as projections of interior volumes. I endeavoured to express every swelling of torso and limbs, the efflorescence of a muscle or bone extending deep under the skin. And so the truth of my figures, instead of being superficial, seems to blossom forth from within like life itself.' [22]

22-23. A. Rodin - Gsell, p. 46.

This technique gives his sculptures 'at once their vigour and their vibrant suppleness.' [23]

While seeking the best means of achieving living art, Rodin never deviated from the aim of his artistic creation : man, and the expression of the inner truth.

To Rodin 'beauty in art is solely expressive truth. He who foolishly tries to prettify what he

24. Paul Gsell : Chez Rodin, l'Art et les Artistes, nr. 109, 1914, p. 66.

sees, to mask the ugliness seen in reality or hide the sadness it contains, he will truly meet with ugliness in art, that is the inexpressive.' [24]

This concept of beauty, ranging beyond the ideal of perfect form, widens considerably the scope of art. Nothing that is human is alien to the artist. Suffering, misery, terror, the torments of the soul and the deformities they cause interest him equally as much as the harmony of proportions, for they express human truth.

To be true is to understand Nature and her laws and follow her example, so as to create forms that have a life of their own. Truth is not exactness, but the sincere expression of an artist's feeling in the face of reality. To achieve such truth, he must be free, able to see the world through his own eyes with 'uncompromising frankness' : a piercing look that reveals 'the hidden meaning of all things', 'the inner truth reflected in the outer truth'. For art precludes all slavish copying of the visible world so as to reach the essence of things.

By spiritual communion with Nature, the artist can attain the inner truth which is the expression of being.

25. A. Rodin - Paul Gsell, p. 37.

'An artist is Nature's confidant', said Rodin. 'Trees and plants talk to him like friends.' [25] This language of friendship can only be understood by discerning the particular character of each thing and its tendency to universality.

Character defines identity; the tendency to universality expresses the aspiration of every living thing to partake of the general laws of life, and be integrated in Nature as a whole. This duality of separation and integration is found everywhere as one of the essential conditions of being.

'Everything in Nature has character, Rodin said. 'Character is the vital truth of any spectacle, ugly or beautiful. In art, only that which has character has beauty. What is ugly in art is that which is false, artificial, trying to be pretty or handsome instead of being expressive, that which is genteel and affected, which smiles for no reason, is mannered without cause, all that is show of beauty or grace, all that lies.' [26]

This is the most outright rejection of the theories of the academic school, who saw art as an illusion designed to make life more bearable by showing the image of an ideal world that would make us forget the miseries of everyday existence.

For Rodin, art is not a way of escape, but one of the paths to a deep knowledge of reality; which is why his contemporaries called him 'the Zola of sculpture.'

The cult of truth is always related to man. Rodin's humanism puts man in the centre of his work.

The *Gates of Hell* is the drama of mankind, shown in the torments of the flesh and of the soul. The greater part of this composition belongs to the cycle of the evolution of human consciousness, which is the main theme of his work.

The cycle began in 1877 with *The Age of Bronze* showing the awakening of consciousness in Man's first confrontation with Nature. *Adam* is awareness of sin, while *St. John the Baptist preaching* is active consciousness expressed in the Word. With *The Burghers of Calais,* Rodin reaches the stage of collective awareness which, through solidarity and self-denial, saves the community. *The Thinker* is Man who has evolved to solitude, meditating as he faces his destiny : he is strong and powerful,

26. A. Rodin - Gsell, p. 35
36.

for his strength rests on his ability to think the world. At the apex of this evolution we find creative genius, embodied in the statue of *Balzac,* who sums up all the powers of the mind and, transcending Man's estate, looks Godhead in the face. Then comes the decline : in *Ugolino and his Children* we see the abolition of conscience that allows the animal to reemerge in Man. In *The Old Courtesan* we have the awareness of human decrepitude duo to the ravages of time. And then, finally, there is conscience forgotten in yielding to the irresistible call of the flesh and passion (*The Kiss, Fugit Amor, The Eternal Idol,* etc.)

The cycle of the evolution of human consciousness gives us the measure of Rodin's work. It is the story of Mankind, stripped of anecdote and seen as a struggle between mind and matter. From the first hesitant steps of *Man Awakening to Nature* — one of the titles of *The Age of Bronze* — to the pride of genius throwing out a challenge to life in *Balzac,* Rodin went through all the stages of that unceasing fight which is the condition of Man's existence. He asserted his faith in the power of mind that frees Man from the shackles of matter.

Much has been made of the sensuality of some of Rodin's sculptures. Indubitably, he did know how to render tactile values in marble, the thrill of a caress and the frenzy of desire. But his sculpture is never vulgar, for the soul is always present : he so exalts form that it is transfigured;

THE OLD COURTESAN. *Figure from the Gates of Hell. Inspired by François Villon's poem La Vieille Heaulmière, Rodin here expresses with great concern for truth the sadness, weariness and decrepitude of old age.*

22

he rises above mere sensuality and the particular case by the power of generalisation and the intensity of plastic expression.

Concern for truth in Rodin is always coupled with the urge to approach the essence of things. How can this be attained if not by passion ?

'The great point is to feel, to love, to hope, to thrill, to live, to be a man before being an artist', Rodin wrote in his Artistic Testament. 'Art is only feeling. But without the knowledge of volumes, proportions and colours, without manual skill, the most vivid feeling is paralyzed.' [27] In these words we find the three basic factors of Rodin's art : feeling, the science of sculptured form, and mastery of execution.

27. A. Rodin - Paul Gsell, p. 201.

By close observation of reality, the artist discovers the laws of Nature, the fundamental patterns that contain all forms.

'I have come to realise that geometry is at the bottom of sentiment or rather that each expression of sentiment is made by a movement governed by geometry. Geometry is everywhere present in Nature. A woman combing her hair goes through a series of rhythmic movements which constitute a beautiful harmony. The entire rhythm of the body is governed by law... Nature is the supreme architect. Everything is built in the finest equilibrium; and everything too is enclosed in a triangle or a cube or some modification of them. I have adopted this principle in building up my statuary,

MORNING – *Toilet of Venus – marble. National Gallery of Art, Washington. This maidenly form has the radiance of living flesh : animated by quivering vaporous half-tones and transitions so finely shaded they seem to dissolve into air, it has the exquisite charm of youth triumphant.*

28. *Conversations with Rodin, in F. Lawton, p. 156, and J. Cladel, p. 401.*

simplifying and restraining always in the organisation of the parts so as to give the whole a greater unity... Cubic reason is the mistress of things, not appearance.'[28]

A work of art is not the spontaneous product of inspiration but a balanced composition in which integrity of form, rhythm and proportions play the main part. The artist may intervene to amplify certain parts, to emphasize others, to exaggerate the characteristic features which determine sculptural expression. But all these interventions are subordinated to the active equilibrium of the whole, to the well combined geometrical composition. For a sculpture is a volume that lives in space or can create its own space.

Rodin has told how he worked on his admirable portraits, and his analysis will help to understand his knowledge of sculptural form and his manner of creating.

'In working on a bust, or in fact on any figure, I always carefully model by profiles, not from a merely front view. It gives depth and solidity, the volume, in fine, and its location in space. I do this however with a line that starts from one's own brain. I mean that I note the deviation of the head from the oval type. In one, the forehead bulges out over the rest of the face, in another, the lower jaw bulges out in contrast with the receding forehead. With this line of deviation established, I unite all the profiles and thus get the life-like form. Those who wish to penetrate into some of the invariable rules Nature follows in composing, should observe her opposition of a flat to a round, the one being the foil of the other. They should also notice her gradations and contrasts of light producing colour in the real object and

THE PAIN—*marble. With incomparable skill, Rodin is able to express human suffering without detracting from the beauty of profile or the thrill of living form.*

should be careful not to produce effects that are out of accordance with the natural ones... In the clay or marble, it must be by the positive magnifying of the material part, not especially by size, but by the line, by the direction, the depth, the length of its curve, that the expression is made equivalent.' [29]

This profound knowledge governing his compositions was accompanied by a wonderful mastery of execution. All who saw him at work were

29. Conversations with Rodin, in F. Lawton, p. 163.

astounded at the sureness and skill with which he kneaded the clay. He had an exceptional ability to master matter, to impose his will upon it, while still respecting its structure. But these results were not achieved without agonised struggle, steadfast and unrelenting effort.

Rodin had two battles to fight. One against matter to release form, whose soul he kindled by desperate effort; the other against the prejudices of his time, so that his living art might triumph.

He plunged wholeheartedly into the first battle, for in it he found fulfilment; but the second was forced on him by his adversaries unable to grasp the real meaning of his work.

Rodin never attacked colleagues or enemies. He faced them with his dignity as an artist and his faith in the future. Ten years after the withdrawal of his *Balzac*, he declared : 'If truth must die, my *Balzac* will be smashed to pieces by generations to come. If truth be imperishable, then I foretell that my statue will make its way... This work that was scoffed at, which they took pains to deride because they could not destroy it, is the result of my whole life, the very hub of my aesthetics. From the day I conceived it, I was a new man... The battle goes on, it must continue. *Balzac* is up against the doctors of the law of aesthetics, the vast majority of the public and the greater part of the critics. No matter ! By force or by persuasion, it will find a way into men's minds. Young sculptors come here to look at *Balzac* and they think about him as they go their way in the direction pointed by their ideals.' [31]

31. *Conversations with Rodin, Le Matin, 13-7-1908.*

Not until 1939 was the statue of *Balzac* erected in a public place in Paris, at the carrefour Vavin.

Rodin was right. This sculpture has forced its way to the minds of the public and today is regarded as a masterpiece.

In spite of all the vexations, Rodin did enjoy world-wide prestige during his lifetime. Since 1892, more than a hundred books have been written about his life and work. Poets, philosophers, artists, writers, critics and art historians from many countries have paid him magnificent homage. His writings on art have been published in numerous editions in France, Britain, the United States, Germany, Austria, Rumania, Czechoslovakia, Russia, Hungary, Japan, etc.

In Paris, Meudon-Val-Fleury and Philadelphia, the Rodin Museums still attract large crowds of admirers. His works are exhibited in the foremost Museums and collections in the world.

His immense influence on the development of world sculpture is no longer disputed. So many artists were affected that it would be vain to try and enumerate them; and after they had profited by it, they broke free and went their own ways. But all these different paths had one and the same starting point : Rodin's lesson.

What is this lesson and what is Rodin's place in the history of sculpture ?

Rodin's foremost contribution was to free sculpture from the dogmas and conventions of the academic school, creating an art that is true, human, sincere, impassioned and independent.

To do this he restored the predominance of plastic values. Unity of design, integrity of volume, composition and gradation of light and shade, modelling in depth, the tactile value of form, movement, rhythm and life force were the basic elements of his artistic language enabling him to express the inner life of a sculpture.

'All the beings created by Rodin live and breathe', wrote Anatole France. 'A world has sprung from his hands, stirred by a timeless tremor. This master has to excess the sense of movement and never before him had art stirred and fomented inert matter with such intensity.' [32]

32. Anatole France : La Porte de l'Enfer, Le Figaro, 7-6-1906.

Rodin's second contribution was to express plastic truth freely by creating objects endowed with their own vitality. Parts of a body, limited to a few broad planes, apart from any subject, were sufficient for him to express the mystery of form.

Plastic truth is the supreme law of his art, whose aim is the evocation of life.

By his individualism, attachment to reality, humanism and his way of thinking art, Rodin belongs to the 19th century; he is its spiritual culmination.

But his work also contains the germs of the future : it has the daring, the taste for technical innovation and the spirit of universality, which were to become the characteristic features of the Paris School.

The search for expressive truth, character and the torments of inner life may be seen as the starting point of expressionism.

By declaring that 'the laws of the cube govern all things', that 'geometry is everywhere present in Nature' and that 'everything is enclosed in a triangle or a cube', he paved the way for cubism.

His aspiration to reveal 'the hidden meaning of all things', to express 'that deep morbidness emanating from the obscure', prepares the approach of surrealism.

Sir Herbert Read drew up a list of twelve works which since the end of the 19th century have set the trend of modern sculpture. It begins with Rodin's *Balzac* which 'represents the first decisive separation from classical restraint. The ideal is no more beauty, it is vitality.' [33]

33. Herbert Read : A Concise Histoy of Sculpture, p. 102.

In the preface to the catalogue of the Rodin exhibition organized in 1954 by the Curt Valentin Gallery in New York, Jacques Lipschitz wrote : 'I discovered there all the treasures and all the riches pelled up in profusion. And pelled up is the right word for it : all the technical innovations, all liberties, all audacities, all the intuitions, in short all the elements of an art in the making were there; Cezanne and Maillol, Matisse and Brancusi, even the Surrealists with their automatic writing and double images, and something more — an immense creation. The names of Cezanne and Rodin will live for ever in the glory of eternal light as two geniuses to whom we owe our completely renewed vision.' [34]

34. J. Lipchitz : About Rodin, Catalogue of Rodin, Exhibition, Curt Valentin Gallery, 1954.

In his Homage to Rodin, Zadkine declares : 'In the pathetic picture of the decline of plastic values, then in the gradual liberation and redis-covery of the life of forms, Rodin is the only ardent personality in the second half of the 19th century who holds his own... With Rodin, this ancient language of man is revived, lives and will live.' [35]

35. O. Zadkine : Hommage à Rodin, Catalogue du 4e Salon de la Jeune Sculpture, 1954.

He has earned for ever the fervent admiration of artists by the way he established freedom and daring in art.

The artist's struggle for freedom, that is the real lesson of Rodin, who in the twilight of his life launched this moving appeal to youth : 'The battle must go on !'

Rodin,
his life and work

Force creates charm.
I have charmed force.
Rodin.

The Faubourg Saint-Médard is one of the oldest districts of Paris. Early in the ninth century, it was a little village on the bank of the Bièvre, outside the city walls. It did not become part of the city until 1724, but its fate has always been bound up with that of Paris.

By the 15th century, the rue Mouffetard, built upon an old Roman road, was already Saint-Medard's main street. It began at St. Marcel's Gate, crossed the rue de l'Epée-de-Bois, rue du Pot-de-Fer and rue de l'Arbalète (Wooden Sword, Iron Pot and Crossbow streets), then over the river Bièvre to end on the further bank where tanners and tripe men plied their trades.

At the corner of Mouffetard and Blainville streets, just opposite St. Marcel's Gate, there stood in the 16th century the tavern called *La Pomme de Pin* where Rabelais, Ronsard, Joachim du Bellay and other writers - gourmets did justice to delicious meals. In the rue Neuve-Saint-Etienne-du-Mont, the house where Descartes lived in the 17th century still stands today a few yards from the one where Bernardin de Saint-Pierre wrote the famous novel *Paul et Virginie.* In rue Blainville, Henri 'Murger recounted the loves of Mimi Pinson in *Scènes de la Vie de Bohème,* and a little further on, at 3, rue de l'Estrapade, Diderot spent nine years of his life.

The Place de l'Estrapade owes its name to the Strappado, a torture inflicted on deserters and thieves who were dropped from a gibbet several times until their arms and legs were broken. [1]

1. J. Hillairet : Connaissance du Vieux Paris, Le Club Français du Livre, 1965.

17th and 18th century houses abound in this colourful quarter, where one finds relics of the past at every step. But its special charm is due to the free, merry, dashing spirit of the place.

The *Sans-culottes* of the rue Mouffetard took an active part in the riots that marked the Great Revolution of 1789. And during the 1848 insurrection, barricades were erected around the Pantheon by the members of the Old Oak Club and fiercely defended.

Rue Mouffetard, lined on both sides with booths, taverns, cutler's shops, groceries, butcher's stalls and squalid inns, had a bad reputation in the 19th century. No one ventured there by night, for the toughs were free with their knives.

In this poor working-class district, in 1837, a Norman from Yvetot, named Jean-Baptiste Rodin, clerk in the Prefecture of the Seine Department, came with his second wife Marie Cheffer, daughter of a peasant from Lorraine, to live at number 3, rue de l'Arbalète. They soon had two children, the elder Maria and the younger François-Auguste-René, who was born on the 12th of November 1840. They led a simple life, having no other income but the father's wages of eight hundred francs per annum.

Auguste was a sickly child, red-haired, shy and withdrawn. Every Sunday, he went to Mass with his mother and sister at St. Medard's and never joined in the games of the other children of rue Mouffetard. His only passion was drawing.

'As a child, as far back as I can remember, I used to draw. A grocer, whose shop my mother went to, used to wrap the prunes in bags made of pages from illustrated books or even of actual pictures. I would copy them. They were my first models.'[2]

His elementary schooling was with the Friars in the rue du Val-de-Grâce and he was not a particularly studious scholar. His father, anxious to see him get on, and having a brother at Beauvais, who was head-master of a private school, sent the boy to his uncle's.

'When I was fourteen, I went to live with an uncle in Beauvais. The pupils did Latin. I don't know why, but I never liked Latin, and I have often regretted it; it might have changed the course of my life. Being poor, I might have become a teacher.'[3]

He stayed only two years in Beauvais, as he was not making any progress and felt homesick.

His vocation for drawing persuaded his father to send him to the *Ecole Impériale Spéciale de Dessin et de Mathématiques,* the so-called *Petite Ecole.* Now he could draw to his heart's content all day long.

The pupils assembled in a ground-floor rotunda where they copied 18th century drawings under the direction of Horace Lecoq de Boisbaudran, an excellent teacher. In his study *L'Education de la*

2. *Conversations with Rodin, G. Coquiot : Rodin, Ed. Bernheim, 1915, p. 42.*

3. *Conversations with Rodin, G. Coquiot, 1915, p. 42.*

mémoire pittoresque, published in 1847, Lecoq de Boisbaudran sets out his teaching principles. He claimed that the first thing was to develop the personality of the future artist, teach him to look at life with his own eyes and draw recollection of what he had observed. Though strict, he was loved by his pupils because he took a real interest in their work and shared his knowledge devotedly. Rodin, Dalou, Fantin-Latour and Legros all profited from his teaching.

'We did not then understand as I do now', Rodin wrote in 1913, 'how lucky we were to have such a teacher. I still remember most of what he taught me.' [4]

At *La Petite Ecole* there was also a modelling class. Rodin himself describes his first encounter with sculpture : 'I remember I had been copying sanguines of Boucher. I went into the drawing-from-the-round class. Students were modelling from Antiques. I saw clay for the first time; I felt I was going up to heaven. I made separate parts, arms, heads, feet, then I tackled the complete figure. I understood everything at once. I did it as easily as I do today. I was in thrall.' [5]

This contact with clay, this passion for modelling it to give shape to matter, was to mark him for life.

Taken with sculpture, he did not confine himself to attending classes at *La Petite Ecole.* He discovered the ancient marbles in the *Louvre,* drew from engravings in the *Bibliothèque Impériale* and found live models for his sketches at the Horse Market.

'In the afternoon, I used to go to the *Louvre* and draw the Ancients or to the *Bibliothèque Impériale* gallery of engravings. As I was shabbily dressed, they only gave me what they wanted to.

4. Rodin's letter, in Lecoq de Boisbaudran : L'Education de la mémoire pittoresque, H. Laurens, 1920, p. 1.

5. Conversations with Rodin, G. Coquiot, 1915, p. 46.

I used to look at the books left on the tables by more favoured visitors, for I had an avid mind... There was a drawing lesson at the *Manufacture des Gobelins* from five to eight in the evening; I went there too. We worked three hours on end, which meant 18 hours a week. At the *Gobelins*, they had kept to the traditions of the 18th century. An artist, Mr. Lucas, taught there without prejudice, which was rare at the time. I also went to the *Jardin des Plantes*, where Barye taught... I was there with his son... After looking around, we found a basement, a sort of cellar with walls oozing dampness, where we happily settled down. A stake planted in the ground held a board which served as a non-revolving turntable; we used to move around it and whatever we were copying. We were kindly tolerated there and allowed to go into the lecture-rooms and pick up bits of animals, like lion's paws... We worked like madmen and began to look like wild animals ourselves. The great Barye came to see us. He looked at what we had done and mostly went away without saying anything; and yet it was from him that I learnt most. He was very unsophisticated. His threadbare coat gave him the seedy appearance of poor school-ushers of the time. I have never known a man so sad with so much power !' [6]

6. *Conversations with Rodin*, G. Coquiot, 1915, p. 48.

Eager to learn, a dogged worker, Rodin never had a real master to direct his artistic education. Neither Lecoq de Boisbaudran nor Barye showed any particular interest in him. He learned from them by listening to their teaching and observing the corrections they made in the studio. But he had to solve his own problems and choose those parts of their advice that suited him best.

He applied three times for admission to the *Ecole Impériale Supérieure des Beaux-Arts* and each time failed. He can therefore be regarded as self-taught.

It was indeed lucky he had to discover everything for himself. Solitude is an excellent training for strong minds. It toughens the spirit and stimulates effort and will.

'I have learnt my art as a student learns his mathematics, step by step, and I have solved the principal problem only after solving a good many minor ones', Rodin told his secretary Frederic Lawton in 1905. [7]

7. *Conversations with Rodin, F. Lawton, 1906, p. 161.*

Never owe anybody anything, wage an incessant battle for self-fulfilment, these were the roots of his independent spirit, of his boldness in artistic creation. What working energy this proud, solitary way demands !

'Yes, he would say, I have always worked fiercely. At first, I was sickly and deathly pale — the pallor of poverty — but a burning excitement drove me to work without stinting... I did 14 hours a day and rested only on Sundays.' [8]

8. *Conversations with Rodin, G. Coquiot, 1917, p. 25.*

As his parents could no longer keep him, he had to look for a job. He worked as an ornamental carver for Monsieur Blanche, builder and decorator, then for *Brèze et Cruchet,* in rue Pétrel, and then again with Roubaud, the sculptor. He modelled skilfully the coils, caryatids and other decorations for the fine houses then being built. At the time, Paris was a huge building site. Baron Haussmann, the Prefect of the Seine Department, was laying out new boulevards, squares and avenues connecting the centre with outlying districts. Expropriation for purposes of demolition enriched property owners overnight and the new fortunes found an excellent investment in building. Labour was scarce and skilled building workers were in great demand. Young sculptors easily found work as moulders or ornamentalists. Rodin changed his jobs several times in less than two years. That was how he met Dalou.

'The first friend I had was Dalou... We met very young when we were working for an ornamental sculptor who often forgot to pay us, so we had to part : Dalou got a job with a taxidermist, I with another master who was more reliable.' [9]

While working for his employers, Rodin never ceased studying sculpture.

This activity was suddenly interrupted by the death of his elder sister Maria. His grief was so profound that he decided to give up everything and take his vows. He was received as a novice by the Fathers of the Holy Sacrament in 1862. After a time, he realized that he lacked the calling. He missed his sculpture. The Superior of the monastery, Father Eymard allowed him to take up his tools again and himself posed for a portrait. Finally, in 1863, Rodin gave up holy orders and began work on decorating the *Théâtre des Gobelins* and the *Panorama des Champs Elysées.*

He rented a stable in rue Lebrun which he fitted up as a studio : 'Oh, my first studio ! I shall never forget it ! I had some hard times there. I could not afford anything better. For 120 francs a year I rented a stable in rue Lebrun, near the Gobelins, which seemed sufficiently bright and where I had enough room to step back and compare my clay figure with the natural object, which has always been a golden rule for me, one I have never broken. The place was ice-cold. I still do not understand how I survived.

9. Conversations with Rodin, G. Coquiot, 1917, p. 109.

MAN WITH THE BROKEN NOSE–*bronze. Refused a showing at the Salon des Artistes Français in 1864, this early work is startlingly true to life. "For careful study and sincerity in modelling", said Rodin, "I have never done more, nor better".*

There I carved the *Man with the Broken Nose*. For careful study and sincerity in modelling, I have never done more, nor better... The whole studio was crowded with unfinished works, but as I had not enough money to cast all I was making, I wasted a lot of precious time every day covering the clays with wet cloths; in spite of which I was forever having trouble with frost or heat; whole blocks came off. I would find them lying in pieces all over the flagged floor. Sometimes I was able to pick up some fragments. You cannot imagine how much I lost that way', he said recalling his beginnings. [10]

Man with the Broken Nose, portrait of an old model named Bibi, who earned a living by posing for poor young artists and doing small jobs for them, was Rodin's first major work. It is a very

10. Paul Gsell : *En haut d'une colline, l'Art et les Artistes,* 109, 1914, p. 7.

bold study in which acute observation blends with firm execution. In order to convey the character, far from embellishing his model, Rodin even emphasizes his expressive ugliness to achieve truth.

When submitted to the *Salon des Artistes Français* ,in 1864, *Man with the Broken Nose* was refused. It was accepted eleven years later as *Portrait of Mr. B.*

In his rue Lebrun studio, Rodin was no longer alone. He had found a faithful and devoted companion in Rose Beuret, the little seamstress from Champagne, who was to share his whole life. Fifty years later, in 1913, Rodin told her in few words the deep affection he had always borne her : 'My good Rose, this letter is just to let you know that my mind is full of the greatness of God's gift in placing you by my side. Keep this thought in your generous heart.' [11]

From this union a son was born on the 18th of January 1866, Auguste-Eugène Beuret.

To meet his expenses, Rodin took a job as modeller with Carrier-Belleuse, one of the most fashionable sculptors of the time. Elegant and aristocratic in appearance, Carrier-Belleuse was a shrewd businessman. He had carved the portraits of Napoléon III, Renan, Delacroix and other celebrities of finance, literature and the arts. Orders poured into his studio in the rue de La Tour d'Auvergne, where young sculptors modelled statuettes for mass production. When a Rumanian delegation that had ordered an equestrian statue of the Voivod Michael-the-Brave found the price too high, Carrier-Belleuse settled the difficulty by offering to transform his *Joan of Arc* into a

11. *Judith Cladel : Rodin, sa vie glorieuse et inconnue, Grasset, 1936, p. 292.*

Wallachian prince by adding a beard, a plumed fur hat and replacing the banner with a battle axe. Quite possibly, Rodin had a hand in the transformation.

However, he had a great respect for his master, whose portrait he modelled in 1882, and thirty years later he declared to Dujardin-Beaumetz : 'Carrier-Belleuse had something of the 18th century in his blood. There was something of Clodion in him; his sketches were admirable, though they lost a little in execution, but he was a great artist.' [12]

12. H. Dujardin-Beaumetz : Entretiens avec Rodin, Dupont, 1913.

The war of 1870 put an end to this collaboration. Carrier-Belleuse left for Belgium where he had an important commission to decorate the Brussels Stock Exchange. Rodin was mobilized in the 158th regiment of the National Guard.

The winter of 1870-71 was very harsh. During the siege of Paris, cold and hunger caused havoc. The Rodin family lived in the rue des Saules up in Montmartre. There was no work for artist and the young couple, deprived of a livelihood, were threatened with starvation. But Rodin was discharged because of his shortsightedness and in 1871 left Paris for Brussels where Carrier-Belleuse offered him work. He thought of staying a few months, just long enough to make a little money. In fact, he stayed six years in Brussels.

This was a turning point in Rodin's life. He was over thirty and had not yet made his mark as an artist. Working continually for others, he had acquired much experience and great skill. He was an excellent craftsman and greatly appreciated by his employers. But no one had yet seen his own works which were deteriorating in his workshop for lack of money to make casts of them. The large figure of *Bacchant* was broken during a removal. Another life-size sculpture he had made of Rose Beuret suffered the same fate. He left behind in Paris a *Gladiator*, a torso captioned *Love*, the bust of *L'Alsacienne*, a little statuette of the *Virgin* and many more works he mentions in his letters to Rose Beuret and which he was not to find on his return to Paris. He was continually harassed by money difficulties. Of all the reminiscences of his youth, his poverty is always the most striking.

In Belgium he was to gain his independence. Thanks to a partnership agreement with Joseph Van Rasbourg, he could at last work for himself. He made portraits which he showed in 1872 at the *Cercle Artistique* in Brussels, in 1874 at the Salon of Ghent, and in 1875 at the *Salon des Artistes Français* in Paris. He supplied the Compagnie des Bronzes with models for industrial reproduction. He executed numerous orders that have been given to van Rasbourg : the *Burgomaster Loos Monument* at Antwerp, decorating private houses and the Brussels Music Academy. He did not sign these works for, according to the agreement, all works done for Belgium were to bear the signature of Van Rasbourg. But he made enough money to be able in 1875 to travel to Italy by way of Rheims, Lausanne and Geneva. He stopped in Turin and Genoa and stayed longer in Florence and Rome.

To Rose Beuret he wrote : 'I have three lasting impressions : Rheims, the rampart of the Alps and the Sacristy (of the Church of San Lorenzo in Florence which contains the tombs of the Medici by Michelangelo)... You will not be surprised to hear that from the minute I reached Florence I have been studying Michelangelo and I believe the great magician is letting me into some of his secrets... In my room, at night, I make sketches, not of his works, but of what I imagine as his framework and the various systems I invent to try to understand his methods; well, I think I succeed in giving them that look, that indefinable something which he alone could give.' [13]

13. J. Cladel, 1936, p. 111.

The encounter with Michelangelo's work was decisive to Rodin's evolution, as he confessed in a letter to Bourdelle, in 1906 : 'I owe my liberation from academism to Michelangelo. '[14]

14. J. Cladel, 1936, p. 112.

He refused to copy or imitate Michelangelo's sculptures for he was seeking a much more fruitful lesson, striving to discover the great master's secret and understand how he created.

The extent of his success will be seen in the following extracts from his conversations with Paul Gsell, where he compares the art of Phidias with that of Michelangelo. To illustrate the comparison, he had roughed out two figures in clay : one in the ancient manner, the other in the manner of Michelangelo. This is what he had to say about the first : 'My statuette offers from head to foot four planes which clash alternately... These four directions produce throughout the whole body a very gentle undulation. The impression of quiet charm is also given by the stable verticality of the figure. A perpendicular through the middle of the neck falls into the inner ankle bone of the left foot which bears the whole weight of the body. The other leg, on the contrary, is free, only the tips of its toes touch the ground and it provides no extra support; it could be raised without upsetting the balance. A posture full of abandon and grace... A double balancing of shoulders and hips further enhances the serene elegance of the whole. Now look at my statuette in profile. It is arched backwards; the back is pulled in and the bust swells lightly upwards. In a word, it is convex. This configuration catches in full the light, which spreads softly over torso and limbs, thus adding to the general attractiveness... Express this technical system in spiritual terms and you will see that the ancient art signifies joy, peace, grace, balance and reason.' [15]

15. A. Rodin - Gsell, p. 155-157.

Now for Rodin's commentary on the second figure, based on Michelangelo : 'Here, instead of four planes, there are only two : one for the upper part of the statuette and another contrasting one for the lower part. This gives the movement violence and stress, producing a vivid contrast with the calm of Ancient Greece. Both legs are bent so that the weight of the body is shared between them instead of resting only on one. There is no repose here, but a strain on both lower limbs. The torso is no less active. Instead of flexing calmly, as in the ancient Greek, on the more prominent hip, on the contrary it raises the shoulder on the same side to continue the movement of the hip. And see how the concentration of effort presses the two legs together; likewise the arms, one against the body and the other against the head. Thus is removed all empty space between limbs and thrunk and there are no more of those openings which, due to the free arrangement of arms and legs, gave such lightness to Greek sculpture. The art of Michelangelo creates statues which are a single block... One last important feature of my study is that it is in the form of a console : the knees form the lower protuberance, the sunken chest the concavity, and the leaning head the upper protrusion of the console. Thus the torso arches forward and not backward as in ancient sculpture, which produces these deep shadows in the hollow of the chest and under the legs... In short, the greatest genius of modern times celebrated the epic of shadow while the Ancients glorified light... And if we look now for the spiritual significance of Michelangelo's technique, we find that his sculpture expresses man's anguished withdrawal into himself, the anxious energy, the will to act without hope of success, the martyrdom in a word of a creature tormented by aspirations he cannot fulfill... When I went to Italy, my head full of the Greek models I had so passionately studied at the Louvre, I was disconcerted by Michelangelo. His works were constantly giving the lie to all the truths which I had thought to be finally established. I would say to myself : Now, why this inward curve of the torso, why this raised hip, why this lowered shoulder ? I was deeply disturbed. But Michelangelo could not have made a mistake. I had to understand. I persisted and eventually I succeeded... In reality, Michelangelo does not stand alone in art. He is the culmination of all Gothic thinking.' [16]

16. A. Rodin - Gsell, p. 158-161.

This profound analysis shows what Rodin learned on his first visit to Italy. It is not that his way of sculpting or his way of thinking sculpture was directly influenced by Michelangelo, but his plastic experience was greatly enriched. His ideas matured and his will to create was stimulated. He was now ready to embark on the great adventure that was to lead him to fulfill his destiny.

Back in Brussels, Rodin set to work again, determined to create something that would at last establish his reputation as a sculptor. He found a model whose beautiful athletic body he admired : Auguste Neyt, a young Belgian soldier who was to pose for him for 18 months.

The excitement of the work did not prevent him from pursuing his researches. Countless sketches and roughs from several different angles piled up in his studio. He scrutinised his model by daylight and by candlelight, lighting him from above, from below and from the sides to catch the play of shadows. Nothing must escape this minute examination, carried to the end whith untiring fervour. When the life-size statue was completed, Rodin was content. This youthful figure of faultless anatomy is startingly alive. One senses the ripple of the muscles covering the powerful frame. The composition comprises four alternately contrasting planes that give a slight undulation from head to foot. The bulging chest catches all the light which then streams down over the sturdy loins, emphasizing the shadows. The whole weight of the statue rests on one leg with the knee flexed, while the other foot touches the ground only with the tips of the toes. The movement of the legs is so suggestive that one feels this supple and robust figure is about to advance. The arms, one raised and resting on the head the other stretched out as though holding a pilgrim's staff, complete the movement of the whole.

Rodin skilfully combines here the lessons of ancient Greece and those of Michelangelo. But the statue has neither the calm and serenity of Greek sculpture nor the violence and stress of Michelangelo. It has its own vitality, its own movement

THE AGE OF BRONZE.
Marked the beginning of Rodin's struggle. So anatomically perfect is the youthful form that Rodin was accused of moulding from life and did not rest until the charge had been disproved. This admirably vital statue represents the first awakening of Man's awareness at the dawn of time.

and its own spiritual significance. The shadow of a dream hangs above the upturned head. The young man awakens and, with still hesitant step, advances into life.

45

The first name Rodin gave to his statue was *The Vanquished,* but he realized that this was not appropriate. He hesitated for some time between two others *Man Awakening to Nature* and *The Age of Bronze,* and finally settled for the second which more briefly expresses the same idea — the first awakening of Man's awareness at the dawn of time.

When shown at the *Cercle Artistique* in Brussels in January 1877, it roused keen interest. The *Etoile Belge* of 29th January 1877 reported : 'One of our talented sculptors, Mr. Rodin... exhibits a statue which is to be shown at the coming Paris Exhibition. It will certainly not go unnoticed for if it attracts attention by its strangeness, it holds it by a quality as precious as it is rare : life. This is not the place to discuss how far there was casting from life.' [17]

17. J. Cladel, 1936, p. 114.

Shocked at the insinuation that his work might have been cast from life, Rodin protested and offered to have it compared with his model. The *Etoile Belge* on February 2nd 1877 replied : 'We wish to bring to Mr. Rodin's notice that we did not for a moment think of describing his statue as a slavish copy and we find it strange that he should avail himself of our favourable report to answer the doubts which arose at the *Cercle.*' [18]

18. J. Cladel, 1936, p. 115.

Instead of satisfying Rodin, this reply only confirmed the accusation of faking which was to be repeated a few months later in Paris, when the statue was shown at the *Salon des Artistes Français* as *The Age of Bronze.*

Unable to understand how he had managed to make his statue look so lifelike, his detractors tried to damage his reputation by claiming that he had cast the different parts of the figure direct from the model's body. This process, reprehended by artists, was a fraud which would have deprived Rodin's work of all merit.

'I remember my *Age of Bronze* being refused — they said it was cast from life. Still, on reconsideration, it was accepted, after someone had said : if it is a moulding from life, it is a very beautiful one and should be accepted all the same. I was shocked at the injustice, the infamy of it... I went to see Mr. Guillaume to protest and demand justice of so odiously unfair a judgement. He suggested I have a moulding made of my model and let them compare. The model agreed. I sent moulding and photographs to the Salon : the box was never opened.' [19]

19. *Dujardin-Beaumetz, p. 82.*

A commission of inquiry appointed by Edmond Turquet, then Under-Secretary of State for Fine Arts, allowed doubts to remain about the accusations, concluding that it was 'not convinced there had been falsification.'

What Rodin was unable to achieve by all these efforts was shortly granted him by chance. A young sculptor named Alfred Boucher happened to see Rodin modelling from memory some startingly lifelike little statuettes of clay. He fetched his master Paul Dubois who, seeing Rodin at work, understood at once how unjust the accusations against him had been. He wrote a letter certifying that *The Age of Bronze* was an original work created by a young sculptor with a brilliant future. The letter was adressed to Edmond Turquet and signed by Chapu, Falguière, Carrier-Belleuse, Delaplanche and Thomas.

It was another three years before *The Age of Bronze* was finally bought by the Government.

That was the end of the first battle Rodin had to fight in defence of his art.

Determined not to go back to Belgium, Rodin cancelled the partnership with Van Rasbourg which for some years had kept him fairly well off. He took a small apartment in the rue Saint-Jacques near the Pantheon and a studio in rue des Fourneaux and set to work again to show his creative power in other sculptures. At first he thought that by competing for public monuments, he could confront successfully his adversaries and prove the superiority of his art. Vain illusions ! In most cases the result of the competition did not depend on the real value of the submissions. The admirably spirited *Call to Arms*, which he proposed for the *Defence of Paris Monument* at Courbevoie did not even attract the jury's attention. Failure followed failure with the statues of *Lord Byron, Diderot, Jean-Jacques Rousseau, Lazare Carnot* and *General Margueritte.* Not until 1880 did he get his first order for a statue of *d'Alembert* for the *Hôtel de Ville* in Paris.

To pay his family's keep and the costs of his sculpture, Rodin produced ornaments and decorative figures for the *Trocadero* in Paris and for the *Villa Neptune* in Nice, cabinet-making work for a dealer in the Faubourg St. Honoré, models for goldsmiths and silversmiths and statuettes for industrial reproduction. In 1879 Carrier-Belleuse offered him a job as 'special temporary staff member of the *Manufacture de Sèvres* at a monthly salary of 170 francs and 3 francs an hour.' [20]

20. *J. Cladel, 1936, p. 130.*

48

He worked three years at the Sevres Factory modelling figures, creating decorative motifs for vases and learning the secrets of ceramic work.

Nevertheless his chief aim remained sculpture. Every year he exhibited at the *Salon des Artistes Français* : in 1878 he sent a bronze bust; in 1879 a terra-cotta portrait and the bust of *Saint John the Baptist preaching*, the plaster statue of which was to obtain an 'honourable mention' in 1880.

TORSO—*bronze. This is regarded as one of Rodin's masterpieces for the inner thrust of volumes, the efflorescence of muscles extending deep under the skin, the vigorous modelling. "And so the truth of my figures, instead of being superficial, seems to blossom forth from within like life itself." (Rodin).*

With this life-size statue Rodin proved beyond question that he could model a figure without needing to resort to the trickery of casting from life. In this work there is even more movement than in *The Age of Bronze*, the hesitant step is replaced by a determined tread. The torso and one leg thrust forward, the other leg drawn back, the movement of the arms, and the head turning away from the raised hand, all combine to achieve a balance in suspense. The whole figure expresses 'the gradual unfolding' of a movement. It is the image of a man walking. It is noteworth though that Saint John is represented with both feet on the ground and not, as reality would require, with one foot raised and ready to move forward. If Rodin had copied nature faithfully, the result would have been an arrested movement as in a photograph. His statue seems to be advancing because it represents movement in the act of becoming, in its active truth and not in the frozen exactness of an isolated instant. The dynamic equilibrium of forces, ready to be converted into action, gives his sculpture a striking vitality.

The body, virile in its beauty, with supple and vigorous muscles, is modelled with the same care and concern for expression as a face.

'I have always tried to render inner feeling by the mobility of the muscles', Rodin said. 'In our art the illusion of life can only be obtained by good modelling and by movement. These are the blood and the breath of all great works.'[21]

21. A. Rodin - Paul Gsell, p. 52.

Evidence of this is to be seen in a headless study entitled *Man Walking* and in a *Torso*, both prepared for this same statue. The powerful modelling with its conflicting planes creating dramatic contrasts of light and shade has an undeniable force of expression.

What is the spiritual significance of *St. John the Baptist preaching ?* It is the image of conscience in action. Man has discovered the power of the Word wich governs deeds. Through it he reaches a new stage in the evolution of civilization.

1880 was an eventful year for Rodin. Most important no doubt was the commission for the *Gates of Hell,* awarded to him by Edmond Turquet to compensate for all the trouble he had had with *The Age of Bronze.* Accompanied by a substantial advance, this was to relieve him of money worries for some time, to give him a big studio at the *Depot des Marbres* in the rue de l'Université, and enable him to give free rein to his creative drives.

The Gates of Hell, intended for the Museum of Decorative Arts that was to be built on the site of the former Audit Office, was never finished. For more than ten years, Rodin laboured assiduously at this, the most impassioned, the most contested and the most chaotic of all his creations.

It is not a gate in the functional sense, for it could never be opened. The jutting high-reliefs and the deep hollows that surround them ravage the sculptured surface and prevent its ever being integrated in a piece of architecture. All the laws of composition are transcended by the genius of disorder which sweeps forms into a maelstrom of untamed passion. And yet, the *Gates of Hell* is a world in itself. Most of Rodin's most famous sculptures stem from it : the *Thinker, The Kiss, Paolo and Francesca, Fugit Amor, The Prodigal Son, The Old Courtesan, Ugolino, Adam, Eve, The Three Shadows* and so many others. The last version of it comprises no less than 186 figures !

THE GATES OF HELL. *Detail of the lintel. This hallucinating vision suggests a medieval Gothic Dance of Death. The frantic forms are swept by a whirlwind of untamed passion that belongs to Rodin's art alone.*

The *Gates of Hell* is neither the illustration of Dante's *Divine Comedy* nor a fantastic image of the *Last Judgement.* It is the artist's profound meditation on the condition of man. Hell is not Hades, nor Lucifer's realm. Hell is in the torments, the unfulfilled desires of the human soul.

Much skill and learning has been devoted to establishing analogies between the *Gates of Hell* and Michelangelo's *Last Judgement* or with the art of Gothic tombs. [22] There are certainly some similarities in form, but the spirit is different.

22. *A. Elsen : Rodin's Gates of Hell, Minneapolis, 1960.*

Michelangelo is an architect, a builder, Rodin is not. Michelangelo has a sense of tragedy, which Rodin has not. Tragedy is in conflict between man and his gods, between man and his destiny. In Rodin's Hell, God is absent. Man is left to himself, to his passions and his solitude.

Albert Elsen rightly remarked that the figures and groups in the *Gates of Hell* are physically and morally isolated. This isolation is not fortuitous. It expresses the thought of this great lonely artist who knew the full significance of human solitude.

FALLING MAN. *Detail of the lintel of the Gates of Hell. The extreme muscular tension, the dramatic foreshortening of the body hanging over the abyss, the harsh contrast of light and shade, all bear witness to the tumultuous force of Rodin's genius.*

THE THINKER – *bronze. Central figure of the Gates of Hell. The Thinker is the image of Man meditating in the face of his destiny. Tensions runs right through this sturdy, bent form, whose spiritual life is expressed in the rhythm of the composition and the inner thrust of the volumes.*

It has been wrongly claimed that it shows a pessimistic philosophy. Rodin who exclaimed 'Life, how wonderful !' was certainly no pessimist. While representing all the various stages in the evolution of human consciousness, he asserted his faith in man capable of thinking the world, in the central figure, which was *The Thinker.*

Solitude is the inevitable result of Mediterranean civilization, which has always centred on man. Rodin accepts it whith the proud humility of Pascal for whom the greatness of man is in his ability to conceive both the microcosm and the macrocosm.

Besides, how can one think this sculpture pessimistic when it is animated by such boundless vitality ?

A comparison of Michelangelo's *Thinker* with Rodin's will suffice to show this. Michelangelo's *Thinker* is calmly meditative, sad and resigned, while Rodin's conveys concentrated and tense force. Contemplation in the one contrasts in the other with energy ready to become action. Michelangelo's statue forms a single block centered on a broad descending curve described by the shouders and the arms that cleave to the body. Rodin's follows the rising diagonal of the forward leaning bust with arms and legs so arranged as to leave open spaces between them and the body. Michelangelo's *Thinker* has the nobility and melancholy of a young prince, Rodin's is a workman, a sturdy nude, whose every muscle expresses the effort and concentration involved in the act of thinking.

Now to consider the most dramatic of the sculptures in the *Gates of Hell* : the *Ugolino group* and *The Old Courtesan.*

In the first, the abolition of conscience turns man into a beast. To appease his hunger, Ugolino is down on hands and knees and ready to devour the flesh of his own children. But his body is not enfeebled, his muscles are strong, taut with effort. His features are ravaged by madness. The horror of the action in no way detracts from the liveliness of the figure. Rodin, even when denouncing inhumanity, cannot help but sculpt a beautiful anatomy.

The decrepitude of *The Old Courtesan* becomes by the strange alchemy of art 'a magnificent symbol of mankind.' 'When an artist... softens the grimace of pain, the shapelessness of age, the hideousness of perversion, when he arranges nature — veiling, disguising, tempering it to please an ignorant public — then he is creating ugliness because he fears the truth... To any artist worthy of the name, all in nature is beautiful because his eyes, fearlessly accepting all exterior truth, read there, as in an open book, all the inner truth. [23]

23. A. Rodin - Paul Gsell, p. 36.

In Rodin's view, *The Old Courtesan* is beautiful because of 'the mind that inhabits that monstruous body', because of 'its intense truth.'

The same intense truth is to be found in the groups which express conscience forgotten in the frenzy of passion.

The Kiss is the most celebrated example. The body of the young woman thrilling to the caress, has the radiance of living flesh. Ecstatic rapture seems to flow through the voluptuous undulations of this body steeped in love.

UGOLINO AND HIS CHILDREN. *Detail from the lintel of the Gates of Hell. Driven by starvation, Ugolino is about to devour his own offspring. At the end of his tether, his features are ravaged by madness. But however dreadful the deed, his body retains its vitalness. Even when he denounces the abolition of conscience that turns man into beast, Rodin cannot help but sculpt a beautiful anatomy.*

THE KISS—*marble. This group from the Gates of hell is one of Rodin's most famous sculptures. At Chicago in 1893 the Kiss was exhibited in a separate room accessible only to visitors who held a special card. Those who found it indecent missed the essential point—the spirited beauty of the modelling, the headlong quest of two people passionately in love.*

ETERNAL SPRINGTIME—*bronze— is the image of love in all its fervour. The purity of the sculpture is assured by the exaltation of the forms. By the force of generalisation and the intensity of plastic expression, Rodin rises above sensuality and the particulary case.*

The Gates of Hell is a work both of reason and of passion. Of reason in that it represents an awareness of the solitude of man; of passion in that it raises the language of form to a level of intensity and power hitherto unknown in the sculpture of the 19th century.

THE PRODIGAL SON—
marble. *Figure from the
Gates of Hell. With a wild
impulse, the young man
throws up his arms towards
heaven, imploring an ans-
wer to his anguished questioning. The whole body
participates in this call
from a soul in search of
truth.*

24. J. Cladel, 1936, p. 38.

From 1880 onwards, Rodin began to move in
Paris Society, making useful connections and
acquiring a reputation.

At Madame Edmond Adam's *salon* he met
Gambetta, Waldeck-Rousseau, Antonin Proust and
other politicians. His friend Felix Braquemond, the
engraver, introduced him to Leon Cladel and later
to the Goncourts: In Madame de Liouville's *salon*
he met Guy de Maupassant, Jean Richepin, Henry
Becque, Stephane Mallarmé, Paul Bourget and
other writers.

He was fond of reading and had read widely, ranging from Dante to Baudelaire. He was in the habit of always carrying a book in his pocket and reading during meals.

On Saturdays he was *at home* in his two studios in rue de l'Université. Studio J was 'a room with a high ceiling, an asphalt floor, ash-grey walls, lighted by a skylight... On the turn-tables, on the benches, on upturned crates, on the floor and in every corner were his sculptures. Above them all reared the panels and pediments for *The Gates of Hell.*' [24]

Art· critics, collectors and writers began to visit his studio. People talked about his daring, hot-blooded art and about the orders he was getting for portraits. In 1881 the Government bought the bronze of *St. John the Baptist preaching*, exhibited at the *Salon des Artistes Français.*

He went to London to see Alphonse Legros, his old school friend at *La Petite Ecole*, who introduced him to a group of well-known artists and authors. His new friends W.E. Henley, Editor of the Magazine of Arts, John Sargent, the painter, G. Natorp, the sculptor, Robert Browning, the poet, and the novelist Robert Louis Stevenson, all helped to make his works known in Britain. Legros taught him engraving and it was in his London studio that Rodin executed his first dry-points, remarkable for the precision and suppleness of the drawing.

Since 1875 when he had discovered the beauty of Gothic cathedrals, he travelled around France almost every year to find out more about her medieval art treasures.

EVE—*bronze. Figure from the Gates of Hell. Consciousness of sin inhabits this quiveringly youthful body. The varying directions of the succeeding planes, the movement of arms hiding the bust, and the tilt of the head, generate a rhythm that combines repentance with grace and shame with modesty in an admirable fullness of form.*

25. A. Rodin : Les Cathédrales de France, A. Colin, 1931, p. 5.

He admired the geometry of beauty' in Romanesque churches, the 'stone crown' of old cathedrals, 'those monuments that contain so much ardour... in which both sculptor and architect shaped and modelled light and shade.' [25]

At Chartres, Rheims, Amiens, Strasbourg and Soissons he made drawings used later to illustrate his magnificent book on *The Cathedrals of France*, not published until 1914.

'If we could understand the real meaning of Gothic art we would be irresistibly drawn back to truth', he wrote. 'How true, right and fruitful was the method of the old masters !... The work is full of mystery. It offers much to the patient and simple man, nothing to the vain and hurried; it gives to the apprentice and not to the student; and one day the miracle is wrought in the hands of a modest workman.' [26]

26. A. Rodin, op. cit., p. 8.

He felt himself the apprentice of the master-carvers of yore and as always endeavoured to understand their secrets and accomplishments.

It pained him to see old churches falling in ruins, calling them 'pictures from the history of France.'

'I should like to get people to love this grand art, help to save what is left of it, to keep for our children the great lesson of the past which the present ignores.' [27]

27. A. Rodin, op. cit., p. 7.

He joined Louis Courajod, founder of the *Musée Français du Louvre* in his efforts to create a movement of opinion in favour of these cathedrals which 'embody the great national past of French art.'

His prodigious activity as a sculptor was in no way hindered by his travels and social life. His studios were so overcrowded with sculptures that he had to give up the one in rue des Fourneaux and rent a larger one at 117 rue de Vaugirard.

CAMILLE CLAUDEL. *This portrait of Rodin's friend, the handsome features modelled with loving care, has in it a share of poetry and a share of mystery.*

His assistants worked at his models, transposing them into marble or enlarging them. Jules Desbois, Danielli, Jean Escoula, the brothers Schnegg, Lefèvre, Fegel and Camille Claudel worked under his direction in his studios. He became attached to Camille Claudel who for ten years was his great friend and favourite disciple. The busts of *Dawn, France, the Young Warrior* and the vibrantly, pure marble named *Thought* bear witness to his great affection for her.

BUST OF J.-P. LAURENS.
*Rodin's portraits have the
rigour of a definition: a
few touches reveal cha-
racter and personality.*

28. *Anatole France : La
Porte de l'Enfer, le Figaro,
7-6-1900.*

In the numerous portraits he made at this time —
*Dalou, Carrier-Belleuse, Jean-Paul Laurens, Al-
phonse Legros, W.E. Henley, Antonin Proust, Victor
Hugo* and *Mrs Luisa Lynch de Morla Vicuna* — 'the
imperceptible tremors of the countenance reveal the
inner state and thought. Which is why these
portraits whether rough or smooth reveal secret,
deep and precious truths.'[28]

He was still interested in statuary and soon had
the chance to create his first monuments.

In 1883 the City of Nancy invited twelve artists to compete for a monument to *Claude Lorrain*. Rodin was among them. His design consisted of a bronze statue placed on a stone pedestal ornamented with a high-relief representing Apollo in his chariot drawn by two horses. The whole was to be 'in harmony with the Louis XV style of the capital of Lorraine.'

On April 8th, 1884 Rodin's design was accepted by a majority of one vote. He took over seven years to complete the work, for he was in habit of working on several sculptures at the same time.

Unveiled on June 7th, 1892, the monument was not at all to the liking of the inhabitants of Nancy. The local press published unfavourable articles, saying that 'this unhealthy art of foreign influence shocks the feeling for Beauty.' They found the statue too slight, lacking in historic character, and badly constructed. The authorities even thought of taking it down, and only the energetic intervention of Roger Marx and Emile Gallé prevented this outrage.

Rodin explained these incidents as resulting from his social clumsiness. 'In most if not all the cases when disputes have arisen over statues I made, it has been some slight misunderstanding which has set the ball rolling. In the case of *Claude Lorrain*, it was an invitation to a public dinner which I refused being tired and desirous of escaping further fatigue.' [29]

29. *F. Lawton, p. 145.*

Nevertheless, the monument does have its faults : the pedestal, rather than the too highly placed statue, catches the eye; and the impetuous movement of the horses attracts all the attention. Rodin has not yet acquired the expe-

PSYCHE. *How supple and vigorous is this torso radiant with youth. To a visitor who asked why he had not carved Psyche's head, Rodin replied: :"The head? It is everywhere."*

rience of monumental statuary. This sculpture lathe appearance of one intended to open air.

His second monument, *Bastien-Lepage*, which he made in 1885-89, caused similar heated discussions. It presents the painter 'setting out in the morning through the dewy grass in search of landscapes. With his trained eyes he espies around him the effects of light on the groups of peasants.' [30] This description by Rodin himself shows that he saw the monument as a portrait and was concerned with the personality of his subject, overlooking the fact that from a distance the features of the face would be lost and all that remained would be the character of a volume in space.

30. *F. Lawton, p. 78.*

These two works were excellent training for his third monument, which was to be a masterpiece : *The Burghers of Calais.*

Since 1845 the City of Calais had made repeated attempts to erect a statue to Eustache de Saint-Pierre, one of its historic heroes. Death prevented David d'Angers from accomplishing this; in 1868 Clesinger accepted the commission but the 1870 war forced him to give up the project.

In September 1884 the Municipal Corporation of Calais invited several artists to tender for the monument.

After reading in Froissart's Chronicle the story of the six burghers of Calais who offered up their lives to save their fellow citizens, Rodin realised that the monument would lose its true significance if it showed only one of them. The greatness of their deed was in the manifestation of group awareness, in the feeling of human solidarity. He saw them as described by Froissart 'bare-headed, bare foot, with ropes about their necks, and having in their hands the keys of the castle and the town' trudging up the path to the suffering and death which they nobly accepted. This moving scene, this funeral march was what he wanted to evoke in all its greatness. He was fascinated by the opportunities that this magnificent theme offered.

In December 1884 he presented his first design, followed by a second in July 1885. To help get them accepted, he offered to make the six statues for the price of one.

It took the Municipal Corporation eighteen months to come to a favourable decision and only after sending Rodin a note setting out their objections to his designs.

'This is not how we saw our glorious fellow citizens', they write. 'Their dejected attitude offends our religion... The outline of the group leaves much to be desired in the way of elegance... The sculptor could give more movement to the ground supporting the figures and break the monotony and harshness of the outlines by varying their height... We really must urge Mr. Rodin to modify the posture of the figures and the outline of the group as a whole.' [31]

These objections were reported in an article in *Le Patriote de Calais* questioning the general design for the monument because, instead of forming a pyramid, the figures were enclosed in a cube.

Rodin defended his project in a letter to Omar Dewawrin, the Mayor of Calais : 'I read again the criticisms I had heard before, but which would emasculate my work; the heads to form a pyramid (Louis David method) instead of a cube (straight lines) means submitting to the law of the Academic School. I am dead against that principle, which has prevailed since the beginning of this century but is in direct contradiction with previous great ages in art and produces works that are cold, static and conventional... I am the antagonist in Paris of that affected, academic style... You are asking me to follow the people whose conventional art I despise.' [32]

31. J. Cladel, 1936, p. 156.

32. J. Cladel, 1936, p. 157.

THE BURGHERS OF CALAIS—*bronze. Besieged by the armies of Edward III, the City of Calais was forced to surrender after a heroic resistance in 1347. The King consented to spare the lives of the population only on condition that the keys of The City should be brought to him in his camp by six burghers prepared to die. In this famous sculpture Rodin shows the heroes trudging up the path that leads to their doom. In truth to life the moving scene achieves greatness.* >

STUDY FOR THE HANDS
OF PIERRE DE WIESSANT.

He did nevertheless modify his first design which grouped the six figures in a block, swept along by a single movement. He disposed them in a circle around the central axis of Eustache de Saint-Pierre, moderated their movement, left more space between them, and varied their gestures and attitudes to better define their personalities.

He modelled separately hands, feet, trunks and heads, seeking intensity of expression and individual character. He first roughed out nude figures before clothing them in their humble harments.

He spent most time on the hands. There are hands that pray and hands that weep, hands that question and hands that give in, hands that bless and hands that blaspheme. Violent hands and tender hands, clenched hands and resigned hands. Eyes and lips may deceive. Hands cannot lie !

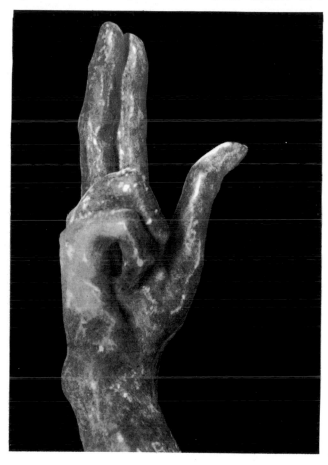

THE BLESSING. *Study for hands. There are hands that bless and hands that blaspheme.*

He shaped innumerable hands expressing the whole gamut of human suffering and anxiety. Then he attached them to the arms they fitted best, assembled arms, legs and torsos — which he called his *giblets* — until at last his heroes took form and came to life.

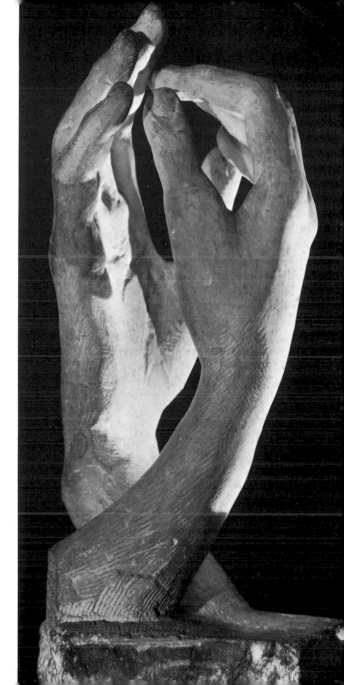

<

THE HAND OF GOD. *The power to create is a gift of God. This thinking hand that shapes a human form is the symbol of creation.*

THE CATHEDRAL. *Hands that join in the fervour of prayer, their slow movement rising like a song of praise to the Lord in heart and mind.*

Eustache de Saint-Pierre is a worthy old man, his bent shoulders bearing all the sorrows of mankind. He is dignified, calm and resigned. Jean d'Aire is austere and proud, holding his head high, his hands clenched, defying death with a supreme effort of will. Jean de Fiennes, the youngest and handsomest, transfigured by the awareness of accepted sacrifice, is turning to his companions

STUDY FOR PIERRE DE WIESSANT, *one of the six Burghers of Calais. The head is like a cry of anguish: a proud soul that has freely accepted the supreme sacrifice and is harrowed by an abyss of suffering.*

to encourage them on their way to calvary. Near him, Pierre de Wiessant, his arm raised in a gesture of renunciation, is proclaiming the vanity of all things. At the opposite end of the group, André d'Andrieux clutches his head in his hands, abandoned to despair, while Jacques de Wiessant tries to drive away from his eyes the image of a nightmare.

Their gestures are not heroic, but human. Each one bears his own solitude, for man is always alone in the face of death. What unites them at this moment of truth is their common destiny; and this destiny each has freely chosen.

The drama flows from the clash of opposites : solitude and solidarity, free will and destiny. Thus the particular case, the historical anecdote is transcended on the general plane of human truth.

<

STUDY FOR JFAN DE FIFNNES, *one of the six Burghers of Calais. How very human this handsome young man dominating his sorrow and calling upon his companions to follow him along the way to calvary.*

STUDY FOR JACQUES DE WIESSANT, *one of the six Burghers of Calais. This is a rugged and sturdy man advancing resolutely, ready to meet his fate without fear.*

The Burghers of Calais were shown to the public for the first time in 1889 at the Monet-Rodin exhibition in the Georges Petit Gallery, and called forth enthusiasm in some and sneers from others In the *Echo de Paris,* Octave Mirbeau wrote that 'the group is more than the work of a genius.' Jacques-Emile Blanche perfidiously remarked : 'I have it from Michel Malherbe — Rodin's favourite pupil — that is was because he despaired of successfully grouping them in any other way that the master placed his burghers on the ground in Indian file, producing this unexpected and felicitous outline... Whether invented by Rodin or simply due to chance, the extraodinary curve of these superhumanly sorrowful movingly plastic figures is so eloquent in itself that one doubts whether a more conventional arrangement would have allowed the spectator to appreciate its beauty.' [33]

33. J.E. Blanche : La Vie Artistique sous la IIIᵉ République, p. 360-361.

The monument, unveiled on June 3rd, 1895, was erected neither in the place nor in the manner indicated by Rodin : 'I wanted to have the statues fixed one behind the other in the flags of the square in front of the Town Hall of Calais, like a living rosary of suffering and sacrifice. They would then have looked as if they were setting off from the Town Hall towards the camp of Edward III and the modern people of Calais, almost rubbing shoulders with them, would have felt more keenly their traditional solidarity with these heroes. I believe it would have been more impressive. But my plan was rejected and they insisted on a pedestal which is as unsightly as it is unnecessary.' [34]

34. A. Rodin - Paul Gsell, p. 68.

Today Rodin admirers can rub shoulders with the *Burghers of Calais* which are placed directly on the lawn of the Hotel de Biron, in Paris. The 'rosary of suffering and sacrifice' remains one of the most moving achievements of French sculpture of the period.

The exhibitions at the Georges Petit Gallery, established in 1882 in a luxurious building in rue de Sèze, soon became the height of fashion.
'The spirit of Puvis de Chavannes, Gustave Moreau and Elie Delaunay together with a vague cosmopolitan Whistlerism and a cautious realism and impressionism led to the formation of societies whose headquarters was the Georges Petit Gallery... The edifice had been built shortly after the inauguration of Charles Garnier's Paris Opera House and in the same marble, onyx and stucco style with gilt coils and ovals. The wall panels were hung with the same brocade as the boxes at the National Academy of Music and Dance... The galleries in rue de Sèze became the meeting-place of well-to-do society. Nothing could equal the elegance and splendour of those nocturnal vernissages where evening dress was compulsory; after midnight the Coquelins Elder and Younger would come with Sarah Bernhardt to do their shopping while sipping champagne. Albert Wolff wrote his article for *Le Figaro* in the head-cashier's office and next morning all of Paris would know when they opened the paper that Bastien-Lepage, Cazin or Helleu were now great masters.' [35]

35. *J.E. Blanche, p. 115.*

Rodin was invited to participate in the First International Exhibition at the Georges Petit Gallery in 1886. In 1888 he showed two of his *Burghers of Calais* and the following year held his first private exhibition with Claude Monet in the same gallery.

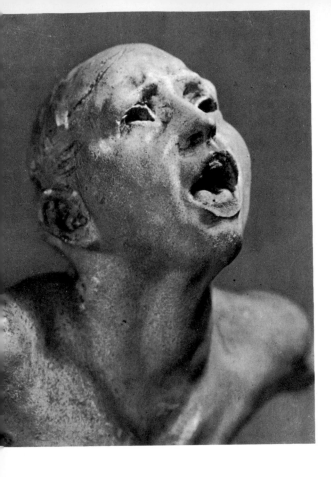

THE CRY. *Rodin shows incomparable mastery in the art of expressing all human sentiments.*

The catalogue contained two prefaces : one on Claude Monet by Octave Mirbeau, the other on Rodin by Gustave Geffroy. The exhibition made a considerable impact and was the event of the season. It consecrated two great artist, so close to each other in their outlook, boldness and spirit of independence.

They were the same age to within two days. They had encountered the same difficulties in the beginning, both had known poverty and privation and made their way by dint of patience, perseverence and hard work. They had the same friends : Renoir, Clemenceau, Octave Mirbeau, Gustave Geffroy, Roger Marx and Marcel Rollinat. Deep affection, true friendship was henceforth to bind them to the end of their lives.

The thirty-six pieces of sculpture presented at this exhibition gave an overall view of Rodin's work. *The Age of Bronze, St. John the Baptist preaching,* the figures and groups of *The Gates of Hell,* portraits, masks, torsos and studies testified to his continuous development culminating in *The Burghers of Calais.* These powerful, tormented, impassioned works had an unquestionable vitality that overthrew all the accepted values and conventions of the Academic School.

Now everyone had to be for Rodin or against him. Indifference was no longer possible, for the basic principles of sculpture were at stake. The admiration of one party was answered by the violent attacks of the other. The battle for modern art, for living art, had been joined.

The freer minds, the more progressive artists and writers took Rodin's side and increased his prestige.

As a member of the international jury for the Universal Exhibition in 1889, he was able to get awards given to artists who were not approved by the followers of the Academic School. The Committee of the *Société des Artistes Français,* on which Rodin's adversaries had the majority, refused to ratify the international jury's decision.

So Meissonnier, Dalou and Rodin resigned and founded the *Société Nationale des Beaux-Arts,* which gave its first exhibition in 1890 at the salon of the *Champ de Mars.*

This split only envenomed the conflict. Rodin was getting more dangerous as he began to carry off commissions previously reserved for favourites of the Academic School. Hence he must be discredited, his projects must be refused, so proving that he was incapable of creating monuments.

The design proposed by Rodin for the statue of *Victor Hugo* in 1891 provided the long sought opportunity for his enemies to attack. The monument was to be placed in the left transept of the Pantheon, facing *Mirabeau's* which was assigned to Injalbert. It represented Victor Hugo clothed, sitting on a rock, with his right hand raised to his brow, leaning slightly forward in an attitude of meditation. Behind him, forming an arc above his head, three Muses watched : the Muse of *Les Orientales,* of *Les Châtiments* and of *Romantic Drama.*

The Committee responsible decided to refuse the design, but the Director of Fine Arts, Gaston Laroumet, opposed the decision. The Committee then demanded many alterations in the hope that Rodin would withdraw. Laroumet however found an ingenious solution : the existing design would be executed for the Luxembourg Gardens and Rodin would be given another order for the Panthéon statue.

Following this change in destination, Rodin altered his design.

The plaster model exhibited at the *Salon de la Société Nationale des Beaux-Arts* in 1897 was sharply criticized. Georges Lafenestre wrote in the *Revue des Deux-Mondes* : 'this plaster group is nothing but a disjointed, incoherent model.'[36]

36. J. Cladel, 1936, p. 176.

The monument was not unveiled until 1909 in the gardens of the Palais-Royal. The statue for the Pantheon was never completed.

Wearied by all these annoyances, Rodin sought refuge in the country. At Bellevue, near Sevres, he found a villa on a hill, in the middle of a garden that gave onto a wood. It was the former home of Scribe, the playwright. Every morning, Rodin went to Paris, either to his studio in rue de l'Université or to the one named Clos Payen, off Boulevard d'Italie, where Camille Claudel awaited him. He was happy to return in the evening to the Villa Scribe, to the silence, the calm and the fresh air of the woods. He liked to take long walks through woods and fields.

'Where did I learn to understand sculpture ? In the woods, observing the trees; on the roads, watching the formations of clouds; in my studio looking at the model; everywhere except in schools. What nature has taught me, I have tried to put into my works.'[37]

37. A. Rodin : Les Cathédrales de France, p. 8.

Every year he travelled through Touraine, Provence, Brittany, wandering happily along the highways of France. He always had his sketchbook with him on holiday, for he hated to be inactive. 'Up to the age of fifty I had all the worries of poverty. I have always lived as a workman but I was so happy working that I could bear all my troubles. Besides, as soon as I stop working, I am bored; not to produce would be odious for me. Rest is monotonous and has the sadness of all things that come to an end.'[38]

38. Conversations with Rodin in C. Goldscheider : Rodin inconnu, p. 9.

But the work of an artist like Rodin is not always a source of joy and comfort. It also carries with it doubts, failures, deadends and researches that come to nothing. The artist bears alone the whole brunt of his doubts. Who could help him in this confrontation with himself, in his endeavours to give matter the shape he dreams of ?

Other people do not understood why he takes so long to finish his statues, never respecting the time-limits fixed. Is it a matter of fulfilling a contractual obligation or of creating a work of art, the mysteries of whose birth the artist and no one else can guess ?

The *Balzac* affair poses this problem in dramatically acute terms.

On July 6th 1891, the Committee of the *Société des Gens de Lettres* decided by twelve votes to eight to award to Rodin the contract for a statue of *Balzac* to be completed within eighteen months. The other bids were from Falguière, Paul Dubois and Anatole Marquet de Vasselot.

On two occasions — December 6th, 1892 and June 15th, 1893 — the *Société des Gens de Lettres* pressed Rodin to deliver his work, as the term had expired.

The statue was still not ready in September 1894 when the scandal broke out. Several members of the Committee demanded that the contract be cancelled. The Chairman, Jean Aicard, refused and, being outvoted, resigned, followed by Gabriel Toudouze, Hector Malot, Marcel Prévost, de Saint-Arroman, de Braisine and Pierre Noel.

A war of words began in the Press. Emile Bergerat in the *Echo de Paris* and Séverine in

Le Journal defended an artist's right to let his work mature beyond the stipulations of a contract.

Alfred Duquet in *Le Temps* retorted : 'The sculptor keeps showing us strange models which he doesn't like — I quite believe him ! — and which he destroys as fast as he makes them. This game of Aunt Sally does not satisfy the Committee, especially when most competent people, artists, journalists and Fine Arts officials tell them that Mr. Rodin will never be able to deliver a statue.' [39]

The aim of the campaign is thus made clear : to substantiate the charge that Rodin did not have the necessary talent for monumental statuary.

In the *Echo de Paris,* Aurelien Scholl did not beat about the bush : The statue of *Balzac* is eluding Rodin just as a five-act play eluded Balzac.' [40]

A note in *Le Temps* of November 28th, 1894 relates the whole incident : 'When Rodin showed his model to the Committee supervising the execution of the statue, the design gave rise to much criticism. Some said he had made Balzac into a wrestler, others thought a Court jester. All saw it as a horribly misshapen, potbellied, terribly disfigured creature. In answer to these objections the artist recognized his error and started all over again. Not once, but three, four or ten times ; not one of his designs was satisfactory. Meanwhile time was running out and the expenses were piling up ; the *Société des Gens de Lettres* advanced another 5 000 francs to the artist and gave him extra time to finish his work.'

This note, obviously intended to be unfavourable to Rodin, nevertheless testifies to his perseverence, artistic conscientiousness and the extent of his efforts to achieve something really valid. That he made three, four or ten models, and even more,

39. Le Temps, 29-11-1894.

40. L'Echo de Paris, 28-8-1896.

without being discouraged in his eager pursuit, is all to his credit.

The note goes on to say : 'A compromise was agreed between the attorneys of the two parties. The advance of 10 000 francs is to be held in trust by Mr. Champetier de Ribes, the Society's attorney... No time limit has been fixed for completion of the work by Mr. Rodin. The Society declares that it relies entirely on Mr. Rodin's word and he undertakes to complete as soon as possible a work to which he intends to devote all his attention and which demands considerable labour.'[41]

41. Le Temps, 28-11-1894.

Eighteen months after this agreement had frustated Rodin's enemies in their attempts to get the contract cancelled and the work given to one of their own favourites, the statue was still not finished and a new press campaign was hatched.

On August 19th, 1896, *Le Temps* announced that 'several subscribers to the *Balzac* monument have sent a petition to the *Société des Gens de Lettres* demanding within one year either the statue or the refund of their money.'

On August 23rd, 1896, the *Echo de Paris* declared : 'This demand is a farce. The *Société des Gens de Lettres* have received nothing.' Articles for and against Rodin appeared continually in the press, so much so that in August 30th, 1896, Octave Mirbeau wrote in *Le Journal* : 'They prefer Mr. Marquet de Vasselot to Rodin. That is the real reason for the campaigns against him in the press from time to time.

Anatole Marquet de Vasselot, whose marble bust of *Balzac*, made in 1875, is still to be seen in the foyer of the *Comédie Française,* was a member of the *Société des Gens de Lettres,* having written a 'History of the Portrait in France.' He was 'very

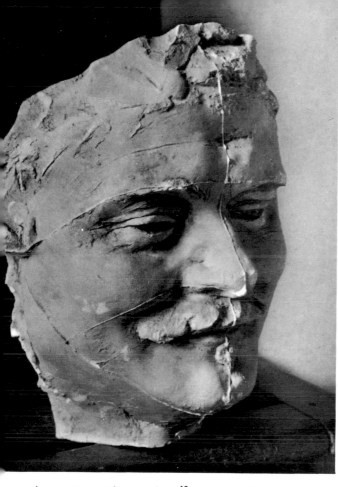

Study for the head of Balzac, smiling.

clever at getting orders'[42] and could not forgive Rodin for having won the contract for the statue of *Balzac.* He had very useful connections in the press, at the Institute and in the Government, and still hoped to get even with Rodin. He was aided and abetted in this conspiracy by 'René de Saint-Marceaux, influential in society, at the *Cercle*

42. *St. Lami : Dictionnaire des Sculpteurs de l'Ecole Française au XIXe siècle, Champion, 1921, vol. IV, p. 343.*

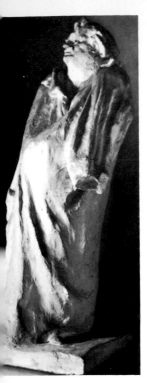

STUDY FOR BALZAC –
plaster.

43. *J.E. Blanche, p. 356.*

44. *A. Flament, La Presse,
19-5-1898.*

45. *Visions de notre heure,
in L'Echo de Paris, 27-5-
1898 and Olivier Merson,
in le Monde Illustré, May
1898.*

46. *Mathias Morhardt
fought a duel with Thie-
bault-Sissons.*

de l'Union Artistique and in committees, a wealthy collector, archeologist and traveller who led an unrelenting campaign against Rodin.[43]

When, after seven years of tireless searching, the plaster cast of *Balzac* was at last exhibited at the *Salon de la Société Nationale des Beaux-Arts,* all the pent-up hatred of Rodin burst forth with unheard-of violence.

Never in the history of art has a piece of sculpture been fought over more fiercely. This was no discussion : it was invective and insults, denigration and insinuation. Criticism yielded place to outrage, judgement to sarcasm.

An alleged admirer of Rodin's incited the public 'to take a pickaxe and smash the shameful block to pieces.'[44]

The most unlikely terms were used to describe the statue : 'that spongelike face, with that vascular gibbosity called a neck, that tin-tadpolish ensemble', 'this heap of plaster hicked and punched together, a monument of insanity and impotence, the brazen act of some Master of Hoax.'[45]

Henri Rochefort, Félicien Champsaur, Jean Rameau, Philippe Gille and Pierre Gauthiez took public positions against the statue, while Georges Rodenbach, Camille Mauclair, Robert de la Sizeranne, Gustave Kahn and Louis de Fourcaud declared in favour. The artistic and literary world was divided into frantically warring camps. Duels were fought between opponents and supporters of Rodin.[46]

Egged on by the press, the public went to the Salon to see this controversial statue and demonstrated against it.

The Committee of the *Société des Gens de Lettres* published a motion moved by Mr. Henri Lavedan and voted by a large majority : 'The

Committee... regrets but feels bound to protest against the rough which Mr. Rodin is showing at the Salon and which the Committee refuses to recognize as the statuc of *Balzac.*'[47]

Rodin's champions lost no time in retaliating. Roger Marx, Arsène Alexandre, Emile Bergerat and André Fontainas spoke out against this outrageous decision. Rodin's assistants declared that 'it strikes a blow at the whole body of French sculptors.' A more energetic protest gained the support of numerous personalities : it expressed, the hope that the people of so noble and refined a country as France will never cease to show Rodin the appreciation and the respect to which his personal integrity and admirable achievements entitle him.'[48]

The signatories include painters (Claude Monet, Toulouse-Lautrec, Paul Signac, Eugène Carrière, Henri Cros), composers (Claude Debussy, Vincent d'Indy) novelists, playwrights and poets (Anatole France, Octave Mirbeau, Jules Renard, Courteline, Henry Becque, Pierre Louys, Paul Fort, Henri de Regnier, Jean Moréas) actors like Lucien Guitry and Lugné-Poe, politicians such as Georges Clemenceau, etc, etc... But only three sculptors were among them, Constantin Meunier, Bourdelle and Maillol. All the others preferred to abstain.

On May 30th, 1898, *Le Journal* — with a very direct allusion to the Dreyfus affair which had French public opinion in a turmoil at the time — published a violent diatribe attacking Rodin's friends, denouncing 'the White Terror organized by the Syndicate of admiration-at-any-cost, of provocation even, about the Rodin of Balzac, not the Balzac of Rodin, Rodin who has become the Michelangelo of the goitre. The Panic-Syndicate writes, examines, acts, fusses and frets, littering Paris

47. La Question Rodin à la Société des Gens de Lettres in l'Echo de Paris, 12-6-1898.

48. J. Cladel, 1936, p. 215.

and the province with its libels while its members scurry from morning till night around studios and behind scenes, through salons, newspaper offices and cafés, for the mass mobilization of volunteers, the Sacred Love of the Rodinians.'[49]

49. Note in Le Journal 30-5-1898 signed Restif de la Bretonne.

The great art collector Auguste Pellerin and Edmond Picard on behalf of a group of Belgian admirers offered to buy the statue rejected by the *Société des Gens de Lettres.* A public subscription was opened to erect the statue in a public square in Paris.

Rodin stopped the collection, refused all offers and said : 'I firmly intend to remain sole owner of my work.'[50]

50. J. Cladel, op. cit., p. 218.

To put an end to the conflict, Rodin cancelled the contract, removed his *Balzac* from the Salon and had it transported to the *Villa des Brillants* at Meudon, which he had bought in 1897. There, in the silence of twilight, he contemplated his work and was reassured : yes, it was an accomplishment which would not be recognised until later, very much later, for it was too far ahead of its time.

The battle over *Balzac* had two aspects : the conflict of interests and the conflict of ideas.

The first soon turned to Rodin's advantage. The unsought publicity increased the number of his patrons considerably. Collectors from every country fought for his sculptures. His prestige radiated far beyond the frontiers of France. In the United States, Britain, Belgium, Holland, Germany and Sweden, the campaign against him was followed with keen interest and the ranks of his admirers expanded strongly.

In 1901 Edward Steichen took some excellent photographs of *Balzac* on the hill of Meudon-Val-Fleury, and published them in the New York magazine Camera Work.

Anatole Marquet de Vasselot and his friends, who had gone to such lenghts to eliminate a dangerous rival, had nothing to show for their pains. The commission for the statue of *Balzac* went to Falguière. The monument which resulted was a poor thing, distressingly commonplace : it stands in the Avenue de Friedland.

Later, towards the end of his life, Falguière was to tell his students : 'I was wrong. I have always been wrong. He was right !'[51]

51. J. Cladel, 1936, p. 225.

The conflict of ideas did not reveal its consequences immediately. The statue of *Balzac* was far too revolutionary to be understood at the end of the last century, when sculpture was much less advanced than painting. It served as a manifesto of modern art.

'For me *Balzac* was a stirring point of departure and because its action is not limited to myself, because it is a lesson and an axiom in itself, people are still fighting over it and will go on fighting for a long time to come', declared Rodin in 1908.[52]

52. Le Matin, 13-7-1908.

What new contribution does it make ? The statue is no longer seen as an imitation of the human figure, but as an object that exists through its own plastic values.

Released from all bondage to the model, sculpture can freely create objects with lives of their own. Plastic truth abolishes the exactness of imitation. It simplifies, eliminates everything superfluous, emphasizes, exaggerates, amplifies until a form is achieved that can live in space according to its own inner demands.

Those who sought a faithful description of anatomy or of a face in Rodin's *Balzac,* according to the classical tenets, were right to be disappointed. Their mistake was in failing to see that this form was sufficient unto itself and rendered Balzac's genius far more expressively.

Herbert Read has shown that at the same period, Medardo Rosso had tried a similar experiment in his groupe *Conversation in a Garden*[53]. And indeed, the outline of the figure on the far left of this group resembles that of *Balzac,* though it lacks the force and movement that give Rodin's work its air of a symbol. Medardo Rosso's sculpture was made prior to Rodin's and the two artists did meet in Paris, but there is no evidence of any direct influence of one upon the other.

The statue of *Balzac* is the culmination of a long evolution. The further he advanced in his career, the more Rodin rid himself of all the superfluous accessories so highly prized by the Academic School, and tended towards expressive simplification. Clothing, for instance, merges in the mass and sheds detail ; plastic values take precedence over concern for psychological expression ; and Rodin's sculpture breaks away from the problems of representation.

53. Herbert Read : A Concise History of Modern Sculpture, Thames & Houston, p. 22.

DETAIL OF BALZAC. *The essential idea of this monument is the challenge that the pride of genius throws out to life. The impetuous movement of the drapery unfolds is a broad rising curve that continues with the hair and ends by describing an immense question-mark. The fullness of form achieves greatness. No truer or more striking image has ever been given of the genius of Balzac.*

Balzac forms a block. Its lines of force are inner thrusts of the material which rises towards the summit through a succession of planes.

Nothing is more immutable than this form, as solid as a menhir, defying the erosion of time. Yet an irresistible drive, a powerful movement breathes life into the tormented matter and endows it with dazzling vitality. Like lava stirred by the mysterious forces of the earth. The planes call out and respond one to the other, they join and sweep each other along, impelled by inner necessity, offering to light and shade the partition of their spiritual music.

For *Balzac* is not only a superb piece of sculpture. It has a spiritual meaning, it is the incarnation of genius surpassing the condition of man. Awareness in its highest form : Man vies with the Gods in his power to create life.

And so the evolutionary cycle of human awareness reaches fulfilment in the statue of *Balzac.*

This object, asserting its physical existence with brutal force, and its spiritual meaning in the mysterious idiom of plastic values, could not but be a challenge in its time.

The conflict of ideas it aroused was fully justified. Two conceptions of art met head-on : one having all the prestige of the past, the other turning towards the future.

Rodin said : 'The statue of *Balzac* is a decisive step towards open-air sculpture.'[54]

It was to be a decisive step towards modern sculpture in the 20th century.

54. A. Rodin : Les Cathédrales de France, p. 165.

THE STATUE OF BALZAC *is Rodin's masterpiece. In its boldness and vitality it opens the way to modern sculpture.*

An avenue lined with chestnut-trees leads to the *Villa des Brillants,* which stands at the top of a hill with a magnificent view over the Seine valley. All around, the slopes are covered with gardens and orchards.

In this stately home, brick walls bordered with white stone, Rodin was to spend the last twenty years of his life.

His neighbour Antoine Grefuelhe, dairy-farmer on Meudon heights, sent his carriage every morning to take him down to the station at Meudon-Val-Fleury to catch the 11 o'clock train. The carriage was waiting in the evening to take him home. Often on Sundays, Rodin would drive with Rose Beuret to the little inn at Malabry on the edge of the Verrières woods, or to the *Ermitage de Villebon,* where the food was excellent.

He liked entertaining at the *Villa des Brillants* such friends as Gustave Geffroy, who in 1892 published the first book on Rodin's work ; O. Mirbeau and Roger Marx, who had fought so energetically for his art to succeed ; Bourdelle, who since 1893 had been his assistant ; Arsène Alexandre and Robert Maillard, whose writings published in 1898 and 1899 had helped to consolidate his reputation ; Jean Fenaille, who had financed the publication of an album of 142 reproductions of the sculptor's drawings ; Fritz Thaulow, the painter, who has introduced him to Prince Eugene of Sweden, the great art lover ; the Swiss author Mathias Morhardt, who had organised in Geneva an exhibition of Puvis de Chavannes, Rodin and Eugene Carrière, and many others beside.

Prince Eugene's visit was followed by an invitation to take part in the General Exhibition of

Fine Arts and Industry in Stockholm. Rodin sent two sculptures : the bust of *Dalou* and *Voice Within.* The Christiania Museum purchased the first. The second he offered to the Stockholm National Museum, but the Committee refused it as not good enough to be placed among its collections.

BUST OF THE SCULPTOR DALOU.

Prince Eugene, shocked, wrote a letter of apology to Rodin, fifteen Swedish artists signed a protest, and the King bought the sculpture for his private collection and awarded the artist the Commander's Cross of the Order of Vassa.

Abroad as well as in France, Rodin's art often met with the same kind of incomprehension.

Designs for an equestrian statue of *Admiral Patrico Lynch* and for a monument to Senator *Benjamin Vicuna Mackenna*, ordered by a Chilian diplomat, were neither paid for, nor returned, nor executed.

The monument to *Domingo Faustino Sarmiento*, former President of the Argentine Republic, gave rise to grotesque and distressing criticism. The Committee found 'the eyes too small, the hair too abundant, the brow too receding' and the whole too slight for the pedestal.[55]

In a letter to Rodin, Miquel Cane, the former Ambassador of the Argentine to Paris, wrote : You said to yourself : Those Argentines are a lot of savages, It will be good enough for them ! — Not at all. You've been squinting. The Argentines are not what you fancy in France. You said to yourself : I see it like that — and you would not listen to the Committee's recommendations. Bah, a lot of savages ! — I say, my good fellow, what would you think if a sculptor commissioned to make your portrait in marble, bronze or chocolate, would twist your long and venerable beard into the form of a serpent like that of Mr. Moses ? The gentleman (not Moses) might say in turn : It's like that I see Gaffer Rodin ! — What could you reasonably object, for his argument would be worth yours ? Be persuaded by me. Go and sin — I mean sculpt — no more !'[56]

55. F. Lawton, p. 213.

56. F. Lawton, p. 214.

In spite of this insolent letter and adverse comment in the press, the *Sarmiento Monument* was energetically defended by Augusto Schiaffino, a former pupil of Puvis de Chavannes, who published several articles in the Buenos Aires paper *Nacion* explaining Rodin's art to the Argentine public.[57]

In London, Brussels and Prague, in Germany and the United States, Rodin's work was more readily accepted thanks to the keen interest shown by artists, philosophers, and writers.

In 1889 Truman Bartlett the sculptor published in the Boston *American Architect and Building News* a series of ten interviews with Rodin and a few years later the art critic X.E. Brownell wrote a study on him. As early as 1893 the Metropolitan Museum of New York purchased the *Head of Saint John the Baptist* and the Art Institute of Chicago bought the plaster *Jean d'Aire*. But it was especially after 1900 that Rodin's art enjoyed success in America thanks to Loïe Fuller who exhibited her collection of Rodin's sculptures at the National Arts Club of New York.

In Prague, Rainer Maria Rilke the poet, who was later to become Rodin's secretary, and the sculptor Joseph Maratka, Rodin's former assistant, were instrumental in the Manes Society organizing in 1902 a Rodin exhibition, which had far-reaching repercussions. All Czech sculpture thereafter bore the stamp of Rodin's influence.

In 1899, sixty pieces of sculpture were shown to the Dutch public in Amsterdam and The Hague and to the Belgian public in Brussels. This was a prelude to the Great Exhibition of 1900.

The century of national revolutions closed in peace. France was experiencing great prosperity in a

57. *Augusto Schiaffino : A. Rodin, El Hombre y la Obra, Nacion, Buenos-Aires, 24-5-1900, and El Monumento de Sarmiento, La Reproducion individual en la statuaria monumental, Nacion, Buenos-Aires, 25-5-1900.*

climate of economic, political and artistic expansion. She drew immense prestige from her cultural values, admired and followed throughout Europe and the Americas. The literature, philosophy, science, theatre and arts of Paris were world-renowned. It was *La Belle Epoque.*

The Universal Exhibition of 1900 was to bring together all the achievements of science and technology. It opened under the banner of progress. In every sphere, Progress was the myth of the modern world. Science now offered new means for man to conquer space and matter. The automobile, electricity, the telephone already foretold changes in man's existence. On every side, progress dictated renewal. Movement became the essence of life, which was seen as a manifestation of energy. The concept of a stable, steady, finally established world gave way to the notion of a world in flux.

Rodin realized that his art, simply a new way of expressing movement and the mobility of things, was perfectly in tune with the new demands of the time.

He decided to assemble all his works in one impressive setting, but where was he to accommodate a hundred and sixtyeight sculptures together with a multitude of water-colours and drawings? None of the existing galleries would be big enough. Well, he would build one. And so he did, on a site rented from the City of Paris, at the *Place de l'Alma,* on the corner between *Cours la Reine* and *Avenue Montaigne.*

Three wealthy art collectors lent him the money to pay for the building and the illustrated catalogue containing tributes by Claude Monet, Eugène Carrière, Jean-Paul Laurens and Albert Besnard and a preface by Arsene Alexandre. Not one sculptor was among those who recommended Rodin's work to the public. His colleagues could not forgive him his success.

The exhibition, inaugurated on June 1st, 1900, succeeded beyond all expectation. Camille Mauclair, Charles Morice, Léopold Lacour and Edmond Picard gave lectures in front of his sculptures. The magazine *La Plume* published a special issue with contributions from twenty-three artists and writers.[58] A hundred and twenty guests sat down to a banquet organized by *La Plume* at the *Café Voltaire* where Jean Moréas, Henri Bauer and K. Boes paid tribute to Rodin's works.

58. La Plume, special number, 1900.

In spite of some criticism by his sworn enemies, the exhibition had a good press.

In a letter to a friend, Rodin drew these conclusions : 'My show is morally a great success and, as to money, will cover costs. I have sold 200 000 francs worth and expect to sell a little more. Almost all the museums have bought : Philadelphia, *Thought;* Copenhagen 80 000 francs for a special room in their museum ; Hamburg, Dresden, Budapest, etc... Less in entrance fees than I had hoped for, but plenty of sales. From 200 000 francs I have to deduct one-third for expenses, marble, bronze, etc. ; that leaves 140 000 and my expenses come to 150 000. Well, there you are, my friend, and I am very happy to be able to write these things to you.'[59]

59. J. Cladel, 1936, p. 245.

Building costs alone amounted to 80 000 francs. The Pavillion had to be pulled down in October 1900.

'I wanted to keep it open two or three months longer, if only to study the collection awhile where I have plenty of space to see it well. But there are obstacles which prevent — the site which is

60. F. Lawton, p. 237.

wanted. So all things must go, some back to my studio, some to different museums and private owners who have lent them to me. It is a pity !'[60]

The 1900 exhibition paid Rodin back for all he had endured over the *Balzac* affair.

Claude Monet correctly foresaw when he wrote in the catalogue : 'This exhibition of his works will be quite an event. Its success is certain and it will definitely establish the position of this fine artist.'[61]

61. The Catalogue of Rodin Exhibition, Paris, 1900.

Henceforth Rodin was considered the greatest sculptor of his time. Commissions for portraits poured in from France, Germany, Britain, the United States, and Russia. He raised the price of a bust to 40 000 francs. This was an exorbitant price for the time, but it simply doubled the number of orders.

He made alterations to the *Villa des Brillants,* where he reerected the pavillion from the *Place de l'Alma,* laid out the park, and reconstructed the façade of the Castle of Issy with the columns, pediment and old stones he had managed to recover. He also added to his collection of antique marbles. Torsos, *giblets,* adorned his garden and studios.

Celebrity did not change his simple way of life. Despite his advanced years, he went on working every day in his studio, where nude models walked beneath the caress of his eager, insatiable eyes.

'I always have living models before my eyes. Not only do I study them when actually working on a sculpture, but I continually have around me nude models, men and women, walking about in my studio to fill my mind with their forms and movements. Thus, the nude, which for my contemporaries is an exceptional vision since even artists only see it in the model they are copying, is as familiar to me as to the ancient Greeks who could contem-

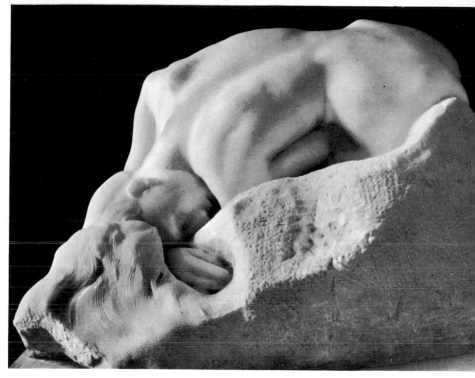

plate it almost constantly at the palestra. I am careful never to impose an attitude on my models; the very thought of constraining nature, of twisting it to order, is repugnant to me. No, when one of them near me catches my eye, I ask him or her to stay as they are a while and hasten to make a rough of what I see... Nowadays, coming to the end of my career, I am content to let them move about as they please. Any attitude that is imposed is unnatural and useless to study. It is replacing the infinite by the finite, interrupting and isolating the secret laws of our being; the body loses its charm and becomes absurd and ridiculous.'[62]

DANAID—marble. The curves are undulating, the finely polished surfaces vibrate, letting the light glide soft as a caress over this exquisitely charming young figure.

62. Conversations with Rodin in Paul Gsell : Chez Rodin, L'Art et les Artistes, n° 109, 1914, p. 61, and F. Lawton, p. 156.

He made rapid sketches, snapshots of life, in which the line is just a wave of emotion. Contours disappear in the blurred shading; the forms are light, open, pulsating with an alluring secret life. Movement is caught in full flight with prodigious mastery. The simpler, the truer are these free drawings that express Rodin's art with such felicity.

BESIDE THE SEA—*marble. Metropolitan Museum of Art, New York.*

THE SIRENS—*marble—Museum of Fine Arts, Montreal.*

The number of his drawings is enormous. At his death over 3 500 were found in his folders. Almost as many were dispersed, given away, sold or destroyed during his lifetime. From the time he drew the illustrations for Baudelaire's *Les Fleurs du Mal* (1886) his style became more supple. His lines are less intense but more suggestive and the light-brown tint of the background has vaporous transparencies which suit the arabesque of moving drawings.

HANAKO. *The concern for truth that characterises Rodin's work is clearly apparent in the admirable portrait of the Japanese dancer Hanako.*

DANCE MOVEMENT. >

63. *For Rodin's connections with dancing, see C. Goldscheider : Rodin et la Danse, Arts de France, 1962.*

He loved the dance, which conveys feelings in rhythms. He attended the performances of Loïe Fuller and Isadora Duncan, the Cambodian ballets of King Sissowak, the Japanese dancer Hanako, Nijinsky and Diaghilev's Russian baller. He made drawings or rough clay figures, fascinated as he was by the young bodies 'which charm force and transform it into grace'.[63]

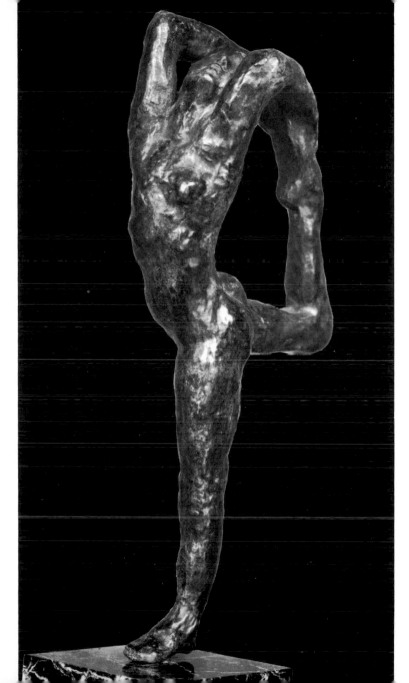

STUDY FOR IRIS, *Messenger of The Gods.*
The boldness and freeness of this movement caught
in full flight are typical of Rodin's art.

He lingered often over a fragment of a body —
a torso without arms or with only one raised leg —
which better expressed the plastic values he was
pursuing. A hand or a torso can be more expressive,
more alive, than a face. He entrusted his dreams to
matter more freely, evoking 'the deep Unknown
which surrounds us.'

He discovered the beauty of pieces of sculpture confined to a few broad planes enclosing form : in this syntax', he declared to Gustave Coquiot, 'grandeur is more the subject than the subject itself.'[64]

64. G. Coquiot, 1915, p. 71.

He approached the mystery of those frozen undulations, those modelled shadows, 'that profound morbidness coming from the obscure', that form the plastic truth of a sculpture.

Despite the vogue which brought him many orders for portraits, his busts were seldom appreciated by his sitters.

'I have never been lucky with busts. Victor Hugo, Falguière, even Rochefort had nothing comforting to say to me... Puvis de Chavannes did not like the bust I made of him, and that was one of the hardest disappointments of my career. He thought I had made a caricature of him... I really thought that Princess Cantacuzene must have influenced his opinion [65]... Jean-Paul Laurens blamed me for showing him with his mouth open.'[66] And Clemenceau would not allow his bust to be exhibited.

65. The Princess Cantacuzino, a descendant of one of the oldest Moldavian aristocratic families, married Puvis de Chavannes after the death of Theodore Chasseriau, whose close friend she had been. She was well-known for her intelligence and beauty and was one of the most brilliant personalities of fashionable Paris during the second half of the XIXth century.

66. Conversations with Rodin in G. Coquiot, 1915, p. 25, and in A. Rodin - Paul Gsell, p. 114-115.

Bernard Shaw tells how Rodin worked at his portraits : While he worked, he achieved a number of miracles. At the end of the first fifteen minutes, after having given a simple idea of the human form to the block of clay, he produced by the action of his thumb a bust so living that I would have taken it away with me to relieve the sculptor of any further work... But this phase vanished like a summer cloud as the bust evolved. I say the plan evolved because within the space of a month my bust passed successively, under my eyes, through all the stages of art's evolution. The first fifteen minutes having passed, he became serious and began a careful reproduction of my features in their exact dimensions of life. Then, this representation went back mysteriously to the cradle of Christian art and at this moment I had the desire to say again : For the love of Heaven, stop and give me that !... It is a truly Byzantine masterpiece. Then, by little, it seemed that Bernini intermingled with the work. Then, to my great horror, the bust softened in order to become a commendable eighteen-century morceau, elegant enough to make one believe that Houdon had retouched a head by Canova or Thorwaldsen... Once again a century rolled by in a single night and the bust became a bust by Rodin and it was a living reproduction of the head that reposes on my shoulders. The hand of Rodin worked not as the hand of a sculptor works, but as the work of *Elan Vital*. The *Hand of God* is his own hand.' [67]

67. See A. Elsen, p. 126.

If one thinks of the considerable number of portraits Rodin made after 1900, one realizes the immense labour he never ceased to deploy right into old age. His last works were again portraits, of *Pope Benedict XV* and of *Etienne Clementel*.

He was content. Enthusiastic tokens of admiration flowed in from all sides. On leaving a banquet in his honour in London in 1902, his carriage was unharnessed by Art students who pulled him in triumph to his residence. The following year he was elected President of the International Society of Sculptors, Painters and Engravers and in 1907 he was made doctor honoris causa of the University of Oxford.

The Kings of England, and of Greece, and the Emperor of Annam, called upon him at the *Villa des Brillants*; the Kaiser approached him for a portrait, but Rodin declined.

PORTRAIT OF MOZART, *based on the composer Gustav Mahler. A nobly spiritual portrait, shrouded in dreams as in a veil.* >

The Thinker was placed in front of the Pantheon and a second cast of the *Burghers of Calais* in the gardens of the Houses of Parliament in London.

The Metropolitan Museum of New York purchased ten of his sculptures to be exhibited in a separate hall.

'I believe I have reached — though at what cost in labour, observation of life and study — a certain mastery that gives me nothing but satisfaction and boundless joy. To think that I have reached this consoling serenity so late in life, when to realize but part of my dreams I would need to labour at least as long as I have till now.'[68]

As he grew older, he became more dour, irritable, temperamental and unfair.

Despiau, who was his assistant at the same time as Pompon, said : 'Rodin was terribly, no, ferociously demanding. He made me weep, but what a master !'[69]

Rainer Maria Rilke became his secretary in October 1905 and was roughly dismissed six months later as the result of a misunderstanding. In May 1906, Rilke wrote to him : 'Here I am, thrown out like a dishonest servant from the little house where anon your friendship made me feel at home.'[70]

He quarrelled with his most faithful admirers, Roger Marx, Charles Morice, Judith Cladel, and yet the battle still raged around him. The last clash was to be over the creation of the Rodin Museum.

In 1908 he had rented as a studio the ground-floor of the Hotel de Biron, in rue de Varenne, at the corner of the Boulevard des Invalides. This handsome mansion, built between 1728 and 1731 by the architects Jacques Gabriel and Jean Aubert,

68. J. Cladel, 1936, p. 6.

69. J. Cladel, 1936, p. 33.

70. Rainer Maria Rilke : Lettres à Rodin, Paris, 1931.

was famous for its beautiful gardens and the parties given there in the 18th century by Antoine de Gontaut, duc de Biron. It was purchased in 1820 by a religious community the *Dames Religieuses du Sacré Cœur de Jésus* and served for more than 80 years as a noviciate and boarding-school for the daughters of noblemen. The Law of 1904 prohibited the activity of religious communities in France and the house was converted into apartments and let to artists and writers like Rainer Maria Rilke and his wife Clara Westhof the sculptor, Henri Matisse, Isadora Duncan, De Max, Jean Cocteau.

It was bought by the Government in 1910 and put at the disposal of the Ministry of Education and Fine Arts, which evicted the other tenants and asked Rodin to leave.

At that point Judith Cladel and Gustave Coquiot launched the idea of setting up a Rodin Museum in the Hotel de Biron. They found many supporters. Rodin offered to donate to the State all his sculptures, his collection of ancient marbles and paintings together with his copyrights, on condition that he should be allowed to live there for the rest of his days. He was prepared to pay the whole cost of setting up the Museum.

The offer was considered. The Ministry of Finance and the Ministry of Education and Fine Arts appointed two Committees to draw up legislation so that the donation could be accepted.

Rodin's enemies used every device to prevent the creation of the Museum. They launched petitions signed by members of the Institute, engineered a press campaign, and succeeded in dragging things out until 1916.

To bring the matter to a head, Rodin added to his deed of donation a clause whereby it would become null and void if not accepted by December 31, 1916.

The Bill of Final Acceptance of the Donation to the State by Mr. Rodin was debated by the Chamber of Deputies on September 16th, 1916.

The Far Left joined the Far Right in opposing it. A counter-bill was proposed, whose first clause read : 'No new museum or art collection shall be created at public expense or in any public building during the lifetime of the legator or donor concerned', while the second clause stipulated that 'the artistic value of all donations shall be assessed by a commission of 12, half of whose members shall be elected by the relevant sections of the Institute.' [71]

71. Coquiot, 1917, p. 150.

This amounted not only to preventing the creation of Rodin's Museum, but further to giving his enemies the right to judge any art bequest to the State.

The sponsor of this counter-proposal referred in his speech to 'the artist who has set himself to shock the world' and to 'the exorbitant compensation Rodin demands in his old age', which drew from Anatole de Monzie the pointed retort: 'We are not discussing a donation *to* Mr. Rodin, but a donation *from* him.' [72]

72. Coquiot, 1917, p. 154.

The donation was then worth tens of millions of francs and would keep in France an artistic treasure which other countries would be eager to get.

The Bill was finally approved by the Chamber by 379 votes to 56. It came before the Senate on November 9th, 1916, and the attacks against Rodin took an even more violent turn.

'Behind the highly questionable genius of Mr. Rodin lurk other speculators', one Senator declaimed. 'Some of these speculators doubtless thought to stir up sensational publicity for sculptor Rodin and, by gaining national recognition, to push up the price of his left-overs and make an enormous profit for themselves, out of the snobery, artistic ignorance and demented vanity of gullible millionaires in both worlds, and more especially in the New World. The Rodin affair is, moreover, an example of the national, intellectual and moral enslavement of this country to a sect.'[73]

Reading these infamies today, one is dumbfounded. They show that Rodin's adversaries had reached such a pitch of exasperation that they resorted without hesitating to the basest insinuations.

The Senate passed the Bill by 209 votes to 26 and the Rodin Museum came into being before the deadline of 31 December 1916.

To ensure Rose Beuret's future in case he should die first, Rodin decided to marry her. The ceremony was performed at the *Villa des Brillants* on January 29, 1917... Eighteen days later Marie-Rose Beuret returned to her Maker. Standing over the mortal remains and contemplating that beloved face, Rodin sighed : 'She is beautiful ! It is sculpture, altogether sculpture !'[74]

He was alone again, bereaved of the affection that had been a priceless comfort to him for over half a century.

Bowed down by age and sickness, he awaited his own end. It was not long coming. On November 17, 1917, he closed for ever those eyes which had looked at the world with such felicity.

73. J. Cladel, 1936, p. 396.

74. J. Cladel, 1936, p. 396.

On his tomb, in front of the *Villa des Brillants*, *The Thinker* bears witness to his faith in Mankind.

Half century has gone by since Rodin's death. In that time, the world has known one of the greatest tragedies in history. Never have human values been so brutally challenged as during these last fifty years. Never has the conscience of Mankind been so sorely tried.

But despite all the horrors of war, all the atrocities and inhuman suffering that have ravaged the world, Western civilization has not lost faith in the destiny of Man.

At a time when life was worth nothing, a great French writer had the courage to proclaim that nothing is of greater value than a human life.

The spiritual significance of Rodin's work confirms the humanist tradition of French culture. By evoking the stages in the evolution of human consciousness from the dawn of time to the summit of genius, Rodin's work expresses the victory of mind over matter.

Straddling two centuries, Rodin's work includes sculptures that have stood the test of time and others that have aged. But an artist's contribution should be judged by his successes, not by his inevitable failures. Rodin's successes have for more than fifty years been to all artists an inexhaustible source of inspiration. All the trends in 20th century art were made possible by the contribution of Rodin, which gave sculpture the sense of plastic values, liveliness and the spirit of independence.

THE SECRET.

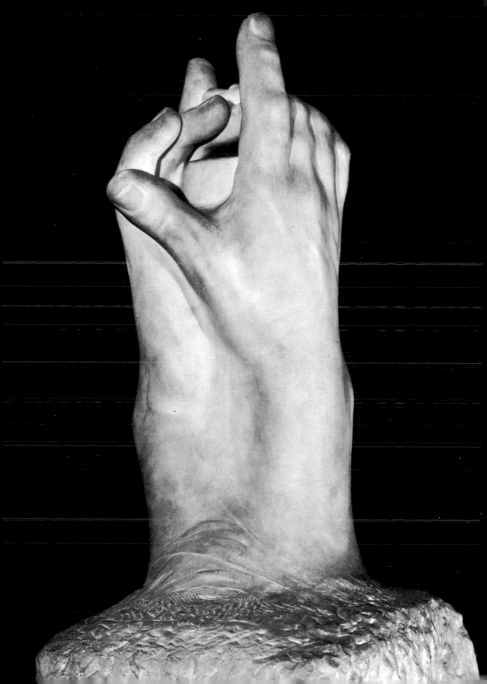

By extending the realm of art to the confines of the Unknowable, he restored the mystery of things and the search for their inner truth. Thus the artist became a true creator, instead of remaining a mere imitator.

Rodin helped his contemporaries and successors to understand that art is an unrelenting battle that leads to the very heart of things where the being finds his essential truth.

In our day, when man aspires to explore the galaxies, Rodin's art reminds us that an immeasurably vaster universe still remains to be discovered in the human soul and its yearning for the absolute and eternal.

Ionel Jianou.

THOUGHT – *marble. Portrait of Camille Claudel.*

chronology

1840 François-Auguste-René Rodin was born on November 12th in Paris, at 3, rue de l'Arbalète, the home of his parents, Jean-Baptiste Rodin and Marie Cheffer.

1847-51 Attended elementary school at the Ecole des Frères in rue du Val-de-Grâce.

1852-53 In private boarding-school run by his uncle Alexandre Rodin in Beauvais.

1854-59 Attented classes at the Ecole Impériale de Dessin et de Mathématiques. Entered three times in competition for admission to the Ecole Superieure des Beaux-Arts and was rejected each time.

1860-61 Worked as caster and ornamentalist with Mr Blanche, building and decorating contractor, then in the work-shop of Brèze et Cruchet, in rue Pétrel. Worked with Dalou at Roubaud's, the sculptor.

1862 Death of his sister Marie Rodin. Entered monastery of the Pères du Saint-Sacrement, as novice.

1863 Carved Father Eymard's bust. Gave up the holy orders. Worked at decoration of Théâtre des Gobelins, the Panorama of the Champs-Elysées and the Théâtre de la Gaîté.

1864 Carved from model the *Man with the Broken Nose* which was rejected by Salon des Artistes Français. Met Rose Beuret who would become his wife. Found a job as modeller in Carrier-Belleuse's studio.

1865 Hired a studio in rue Lebrun. Befriended Claude Monet.

1866 Birth of his son Auguste Beuret. Worked at the decoration of the private residence of La Païva in the Champs Elysées. Stayed in Strasbourg where he restored the sculpture in some churches.

1868 Travelled to Marseilles via Lyon, Aix and Nimes. Worked with Fourquet decorating the Palais des Beaux-Arts in Marseilles.

1870 Enlisted in 158th Regiment of the Garde Nationale in Paris. Toward the end of the year was discharged on account of shortsightedness.

1871 After the armistice, joined Carrier-Belleuse in Brussels where he worked under his control decorating the Stock Exchange House. Fell out with Carrier-Belleuse.

1872 Hired a studio at Ixelles in 111, rue Sans-Souci. Rose Beuret joined him in Brussels. Made models for the Compagnie des Bronzes. Exhibited at the Cercle Artistique in Brussels.

1873	Associated with Joseph van Rasbourg for the execution of sculptures and decorating work.
1874	Exhibited Dr Thiriar's bust at Ghent salon.
1875	Exhibited at the Salon des Artistes Français in Paris and at the Cercle Artistique in Brussels. Entered competition for Lord Byron monument in London ; competition won by Richard Belt. Travelled in Italy via Rheims, Pontarlier, Lausanne, Geneva and Turin. In Florence and Rome studied Michelangelo's and Donatello's sculptures. Back in Brussels, started work from live for the statue the *Bronze Age.*
1876	The models executed for the Compagnie des Bronzes were exhibited in Philadelphia at the United States Centennial Exhibition. Made friends with Constantin Meunier. Carved the figures of the pedestal for the monument of Burgomaster Loos at Antwerp.
1877	In January exhibited the *Bronze Age* at the Cercle Artistique in Brussels under the caption *The Vanquished.* The Press accused him of having moulded the statue from the model. Rodin protested. Exhibited the *Bronze Age* at the Salon des Artistes Français ; same accusations were raised.
1878	The battle around the *Bronze Age* continued. Sculptors Paul Dubois, Chapu, Carrier-Belleuse, Chaplain, Falguière, Delaplanche. Thomas and Boucher sent a letter in defence of Rodin to

the Minister of Fine-Arts. Exhibited a bust at Salon des Artistes Français. Was engaged by sculptor Laouste and worked at decoration of *Trocadero.* Travelled to Nice where made two figures for Villa Neptune.

1879	Exhibited at Salon des Artistes Français the bust of *Saint John-the-Baptist Preaching* and a portrait. Presented his *Call to Arms* in competition for *Monument The Defence of Paris* at Courbevoie ; competition won by Barrias. Was engaged in temporary staff of Sèvres factory, making models for vases, cups, etc.
1880	Got honourable mention at Salon des Artistes Français where exhibited the *Bronze Age,* in bronze, and the statue *Saint John-the-Baptist Preaching. Bronze Age* was bought by the State and Edmond Turquet entrusted him with execution of monumental door for new Museum of Decorative Art. Began work on the *Gates of Hell* which he would never complete. Since 1880 carved *Adam, Eve, The Thinker* and the *Three Shades* which were to be part of the *Gates of Hell.*
1881	Went to London to visit his friend Alphonse Legros who contacted him with W.E. Henley, the chief editor of the Magazine of Art, sculptor Natorp, writers R.L. Stevenson and Robert Browning. Exhibited at Salon des Artistes Français *Saint John-the-Baptist Preaching* (bronze) and the *Creation of Man (Adam).* Gave lessons in

sculpture to G. Natorp, R. Barrett-Browning, and F. Baden-Powell. Made his first burin engravings. Entered unsuccessfuly in competition for monument of *Lazare Carnot.*

1882 Exhibited at Salon des Artistes Français portraits of Carrier-Belleuse and painter J.P. Laurens. Obtained a studio in Dépot des Marbres in 182, rue de l'Université. Gave up job at Sèvres factory.

1883 Carved bust of *Victor Hugo.* Exhibited at Salon des Artistes Français and Exposition Nationale des Beaux-Arts in Paris.

1884 Exhibited portraits of *Victor Hugo* and *Dalou* at Salon des Artistes Français. Hired larger studio at 117, rue de Vaugirard, moved lodgings to 39, rue du Faubourg-Saint-Jacques. Got order for monument of *Claude Lorrain.* Taught in studio in rue Notre-Dame-des-Champs where met Camille Claudel. Was made Knight of Legion of Honour. Presented first project for *The Burghers of Calais.*

1885 Exhibited portrait of *Antonin Proust* at Salon des Artistes Français. Obtained order for monument of *Bastien-Lepage* at Damvilliers. Made first portrait of his pupil Camille Claudel *(Dawn).* Presented second project for *The Burghers of Calais.* Travelled to Italy.

1886 Sent ten sculptures to First International Exhibition at Georges Petit Gallery. His

model for *Bastien-Lepage* monument accepted. Made the models for equestrian statue of *general Patricio Lynch* and monument of *Benjamin Vicuna Mackenna* for Santiago in Chile. Moved to 71, rue de Bourgogne. Made second portrait of Camille Claudel *(Thought).*

1887 Obtained order for *The Burghers of Calais.* Spent holidays at Azay-le-Rideau.

1888 Exhibited *Mme Morla Vicuna's* marble bust at Salon des Artistes Français. Entered International Exhibition at Georges Petit Gallery with two sculptures. Jean Escoula, Auguste de Niederhausen-Rodo, J.L. Schnegg and Camille Claudel worked as assistants in his studio. Drew illustrations for Baudelaire's « Les Fleurs du Mal ».

1889 First personal exhibition with Claude Monet at Georges Petit Gallery. Participated in Universal Exhibition in Paris, in Painters-Engravers' Salon, and in Ghent Salon where he was awarded Gold Medal. Was elected member of committee of Salon des Artistes Français and member of jury for distribution of awards to participators at Universal Exhibition. With Meissonier and Dalou founded Société Nationale des Beaux-Arts. Unveiling of *Bastien-Lepage* monument at Damvilliers. Obtained first order for *Victor Hugo* monument which was to be erected in transept of Pantheon. Moved to 23, rue des Grands-Augustins.

1890 Exhibited four sculptures at Salon de la Société Nationale des Beaux-Arts. Hired former dwelling of Scribe at Bellevue-Sèvres, nr 8, Chemin Scribe. Hired a second studio at Clos-Payen, 68, boulevard d'Italie. Presented project for *Victor Hugo* monument to Works' Commission who asked him to alter it, claiming it was unsuitable to the site. Travelled in Touraine and Anjou.

1891 Exhibited at Salon de la Société Nationale des Beaux-Arts and the Salon of Engravers-Painters. Obtained commission for monument of *Balzac*. Travelled to Guernesey and Jersey with G. Geffroy and Eugène Carrière. Stayed in Touraine.

1892 Exhibited at the Salon of the Société Nationale des Beaux-Arts the marble bust of *Puvis de Chavannes.* Unveiling of *Claude Lorrain* monument at Nancy. Polemic roused about this monument. Travelled to Provence, via Grenoble. First book on Rodin, by G. Geffroy published by Dentu publishers.

1893 Took part in Salon of Société Nationale des Beaux-Arts, in World Columbian Exhibition in Chicago and in International Exhibition in Munich where was awarded second-prize medal. In Chicago, *The Kiss* and *Paolo and Francesca* were exhibited in separate room to which were admitted only holders of special invitations.

Stayed in Brittany at Fritz Thaulow's. Was elected president of sculpture section of Société Nationale des Beaux-Arts. Took Bourdelle as his assistant.

1894 Société des Gens de Lettres summoned him to deliver the statue of *Balzac.* Press polemic

1895 Exhibited at Salon de la Société Nationale des Beaux-Arts. Unveiling of monument *The Burghers of Calais.* Fell out with Camille Claudel. Got an order for monument of *Domingo Faustino Sarmiento* at Buenos Aires.

1896 Exhibited *Illusion, daughter of Icarus* at Salon of Société Nationale des Beaux-Arts.

1897 Participated in Salon of Société Nationale des Beaux-Arts (five sculptures), in International Exhibition of Art and Industry in Stochkolm (two sculptures) International Art Exhibition in Venice (five sculptures) and in Exhibition of Puvis de Chavannes-Eugène Carrière-Auguste Rodin in Musée Rath in Geneva. Offered the sculpture *The Voice Within* to the National Museum of Stockholm but Museum's committee refused gift. Prince Eugene of Sweden wrote apologetic letter to Rodin. The king of Sweden bought the sculpture for his own collection. Publishers Boussod, Manzi and Joyant published an album of his drawings prefaced by Octave Mirbeau. Stayed at Château de Montrozier in the Aveyron at his friend, Fenaille. Bought Villa des Brillants at Meudon-Val-Fleury.

1898   At Salon of the Société Nationale des Beaux-Arts exhibited *The Kiss* and the statue of *Balzac*. The Committee of Société des Gens de Lettres published a motion of protest « against the sketch exhibited by Mr Rodin at the Salon and in which they refused to see the likeness of Balzac ». Rodin's adversaries waged a violent press campaign against this statue. Auguste Pellerin wished to purchase it himself. Edmond Picard requested it for Belgium. London asked permission to exhibit it at International Exhibition of Artists. A committee of artist and authors published a motion in favour of Rodin, signed by numerous personalities. A subscription list was opened to erect monument in public square in Paris. Rodin thanked his friends, removed his statue, declared he wished to keep it and cancelled contract with Société des Gens de Lettres. Arsène Alexandre published *Rodin's Balzac* at Fleury publishers.

1899   Exhibited at Salon of the Société Nationale des Beaux-Arts four sculptures among wihch Falguière's portrait. Rodin exhibitions in Amsterdam, The Hague and Brussels (sixty sculptures). Travelled to Belgium and Holland. Léon Maillard published at Fleury's a book on Rodin.

1900   Great Rodin exhibition in a pavilion in the Place de l'Alma on the corner of Avenue Montaigne and Cours-la-Reine.

In London, Carfax Gallery organized exhibition of Rodin drawings. Rudolf Dircks wrote a book on him. Rodin opened a school of sculpture with Bourdelle and Desbois in Boulevard Montparnasse. *Sarmiento* monument unveiled in Buenos Aires roused severe criticism.

1901   Exhibited at Salon of the Société Nationale des Beaux-Arts. More orders for portraits.

1902   Travelled to Prague to attend opening of his exhibition organized by the Manes Society. Participated in Salon of the Société Nationale des Beaux-Arts (two sculptures) and in the Biennale of Venice. Went to London where his admirers gave a banquet in his honour presided by Sir George Wyndham. Students unharnessed horses and pulled his carriage triumphantly to his residence. First contacts with Rainer Maria Rilke. Visit to Ardenza at Sophie von Hindenburg's where he carved portrait of Mme de Nostitz.

1903   Rodin exhibition at National Arts Club of New York with sculptures from Loïe Fuller's collection. Promoted Commander of Legion of Honour. Travelled to London where was elected chairman of International Society of Painters. Sculptors and Engravers. Three books on Rodin published : one by Judith Cladel in Paris, one by Rainer Maria Rilke in Berlin and one by Briegel-Wassergovel in Strasbourg.

1904 Participated in exhibitions in London, St-Louis, Weimar and Düsseldorf.

1905 Rodin-Monet exhibition in Boston. Took part in Salon of the Société Nationale des Beaux-Arts and in Luisiane Exhibition. Rainer ˉ Maria Rilke became Rodin's secretary.

1906 Exhibited at Salon of the Société Nationale des Beaux-Arts and at Cercle d'Art in Ostend. Travelled to Spain, with painter Zuloaga, visited Toledo, Madrid, Cordoba and Seville. Unveiling of *Maurice Rollinat* monument at Fresselines (Cruse). *The Thinker* offered to City of Paris by public subscription, placed in front of Panthéon. Travelled to Belgium. Book on Rodin by Frederic Lawton published. Made numerous drawings of King Sissowath's Cambodian dancers.

1907 Oxford University awarded him title of Doctor honoris causa. Travelled around Britain. Rodin exhibition at Bernheim-Jeune Gallery in Paris (215 drawings). Participated in Salon of the Société Nationale des Beaux-Arts. Roger Marx published his study *Rodin Ceramist.*

1908 Exhibitions of drawings in New York and Vienna. Took part in Salon of the Société Nationale des Beaux-Arts. Hired a studio at Hôtel de Biron, rue de Varenne. The King of England, Edward the VIIth, called on him at Meudon. A monograph on Rodin by Otto Grautoff appeared in Leipzig. Judith Cladel published her second book on Rodin.

1909 Participated in Salon of the Société Nationale des Beaux-Arts and Salon of Triennale in Ghent. Unveiling of *Victor Hugo* monument in gardens of Palais-Royal and of bust of *Barbey d'Aurevilly* at Saint-Sauveur-le-Vicomte.

1910 Exhibition of drawings in New York. Magazine Camera Work dedicated him special issue. Metropolitan Museum in New York received from Thomas Fortune Ryan a donation of $ 25.000 for purchase of six bronze and four marble sculptures of Rodin's. Participated in Salon of the Société Nationale des Beaux-Arts. Promoted to Grand Officier of Legion of Honour, was feted at banquet in the Bois de Boulogne.

1911 Exhibited at Salon of the Société Nationale des Beaux-Arts, Grasset published the book *L'Art. Entretiens réunis par Paul Gsell* (Rodin, on Art and Artists by Paul Gsell). The State acquired the Hôtel de Biron. Gustave Coquiot and Judith. Cladel suggested the setting up of a Rodin Museum. Project supported by many artists, writers and politicians. Rodin offered to donate all his work to the State and defray expenses involved in setting up of museum. Two commissions were appointed by Ministry of Finance and by Ministry of Fine-Arts to examine plan.

1912 Rodin exhibition at Metropolitan Museum in New York, to whom Rodin offered 18 plaster

126

casts. Participated in Salon of the Société Nationale des Beaux-Arts and at Biennale of Venice. Travelled to Rome where he was offered official reception at Capitol. Two books on Rodin appeared, one in London by M. Ciolkowska, the other by A. Eckermann, in Munich.

1913 Participated in Armory Show in New York. Book by H. Dujardin-Beaumetz *Entretiens avec Rodin* and by Gustave Coquiot, *Le Vrai Rodin,* published.

1914 Exhibition and journey at London, Armand Colin published Rodin's *Les Cathédrales de France.* Journey to Rome. Holiday on the Côte d'Azur, at Roquebrune, at Gabriel Hanotaux's.

1915 Journey to Rome where he carved portrait of *Pope Benedict XV.* Creation of Rodin Museum encountered serious opposition.

1916 On Septembre 14th the Chamber of Deputies voted by 379 for to 56 against, the " draft bill carrying definite acceptance of M. Rodin's gift to State ". The same bill was voted in the Senate on November 9th, by 209 for to 26 against

1917 Marriage of Auguste Rodin to Rose Beuret on January 29th. Death of Rose Rodin on February 16th. Rodin's life ended on November 17th at 4 a.m. Funeral at Meudon, on November 24th. On his tomb, the *Thinker.*

PHOTOGRAPHES :

Adelys : pg. 15, 19, 22, 25, 38, 51, 68, 74, 105, 108, 113, 120.
Buloz : pg. 52, 56, 60, 68, 71, 99, 119.
W. Drager : pg. 109, 110.
Florin Dragu : pg. 47, 61, 63.
Lavrillier : jaquet, pg. 53, 54, 59, 95, 97.
Rudomine : pg. 62, 65, 72, 73, 76, 77, 78, 79, 80.
Metropolitan Museum, New York : pg. 106.
Musée des Beaux-Arts, Montreal : pg. 107.
National Gallery of Art, Washington : pg. 23.

Printed in France
Imprimerie Couilleaux
4, rue Auvray - LE MANS
pour les Editions du Musée Rodin
Paris - Juin 1990.